OPTIMAL DISCIPLESHIP
Discovering How Christ Has Been Discipling You!

NEIL THOMAS DESIATO

Copyright © 2025 Neil Thomas DeSiato.

All rights reserved. No part of this book may be used or reproduced by any means, graphic, electronic, or mechanical, including photocopying, recording, taping or by any information storage retrieval system without the written permission of the author except in the case of brief quotations embodied in critical articles and reviews.

This book is a work of non-fiction. Unless otherwise noted, the author and the publisher make no explicit guarantees as to the accuracy of the information contained in this book and in some cases, names of people and places have been altered to protect their privacy.

WestBow Press books may be ordered through booksellers or by contacting:

WestBow Press
A Division of Thomas Nelson & Zondervan
1663 Liberty Drive
Bloomington, IN 47403
www.westbowpress.com
844-714-3454

Because of the dynamic nature of the Internet, any web addresses or links contained in this book may have changed since publication and may no longer be valid. The views expressed in this work are solely those of the author and do not necessarily reflect the views of the publisher, and the publisher hereby disclaims any responsibility for them.

Any people depicted in stock imagery provided by Getty Images are models, and such images are being used for illustrative purposes only. Certain stock imagery © Getty Images.

Unless otherwise noted, Scripture quotations are taken from The Readable Bible®. Copyright © 2022 by Rodney S. Laughlin, Leawood, Kansas. Used by permission of Iron Stream Media.

Scripture quotations marked AMP are from the Amplified® Bible. Copyright © 2015 by The Lockman Foundation. Used by permission. www.lockman.org.

Scripture quotations marked ESV are taken from The Holy Bible, English Standard Version. ESV® Text Edition: 2016. Copyright © 2001 by Crossway Bibles, a publishing ministry of Good News Publishers.

Scripture quotations marked (NIV) are taken from the Holy Bible, New International Version®, NIV®. Copyright © 1973, 1978, 1984, 2011 by Biblica, Inc.™ Used by permission of Zondervan. All rights reserved worldwide. www.zondervan.comThe "NIV" and "New International Version" are trademarks registered in the United States Patent and Trademark Office by Biblica, Inc.™

ISBN: 979-8-3850-4929-5 (sc)
ISBN: 979-8-3850-4930-1 (hc)
ISBN: 979-8-3850-4928-8 (e)

Library of Congress Control Number: 2025908562

Print information available on the last page.

WestBow Press rev. date: 06/24/2025

Dedication, Credits and Thanks

My journey toward understanding spiritual formation was significantly influenced by a pivotal question my beloved wife, Eunice, asked me during a study I was leading in Isaiah 55. As I was teaching about the glory of God, she asked, "How do you sense the glory of God?" This question, though I did not have a clear response at the time, became a divine intervention, a tool used by the Holy Spirit to guide me toward the Apostle Peter's insight into how each person may partake of the divine nature (2 Peter 1:3-4). It sparked a journey of discovery and understanding that led to the creation of this book. This book is a testament to that journey dedicated to Eunice and all who, like us, seek to become God's children and Christ's followers in the *'way they should go'* (Proverbs 22:6).

As I wrote the manuscript, I especially thought of my son Ryan and his fiancée Meagan Read, my daughter Jill and her husband, Jason DiLoreti, and the beautiful grandchildren God gave me through them: Stella, Romolo, and Emilia. Their love and support have been a constant source of inspiration in my spiritual journey.

I also thought about all the strong, believing brothers and pastors who have forged a men's ministry with me called Finishing Strong that is impacting our community through the message of this book. Especially my Pastor Todd Edmondson, Ben Booher, and Corbin Cross, all of who cheered me on and allowed me to endlessly explain what I was seeing in the scriptures and attempting to explain in a manuscript. Special thanks to my sister, Virginia Lee, and my niece, Robin Doran, who both contributed in practical ways for this book to be in all of your hands. Finally, hats off to Susan Tough, the copy editor of Optimal Discipleship; her editing is the reason this book reads as smoothly as it does!

Yet, the deepest thanksgiving must be reserved for Our God and Father of the Lord Jesus Christ, and the Holy Spirit; without which I would never have accomplished or achieved anything.

May the words in this book serve as a guiding light in your own spiritual journey.

Sincerely,
Pastor Neil DeSiato

(continued from the back)

"…which way to turn, where to go, and what to do. Regardless of what one wants to do in the flesh, when we listen to God and act on His personal word to us, He pushes us out of our comfort zone into the places we'd rather not go, leads us into doing things we'd rather not do, and then stuns us with how He uses us in those situations. I think Optimal Discipleship will move people into that mode. Great job."

—***Rodney S Laughlin***
Translator and Editor of *The Readable Bible*

"You've made an excellent case for spending more time in God's Word. I've read many books and heard many sermons on the topic, but your argument for doing so is more convincing than I've heard before. As an editor, I've read the Bible many times, but now I see the need for more in-depth introspection. Great job!"

—***Sue Tough***
Copy Editor & Co-Author of *The Anointed One*

Keep on asking and it will be given to you.
Keep on seeking and you will find.
Keep on knocking and the door will be opened to you.
For everyone who asks receives, those who seek find,
and the door will be opened to whomever knocks.
Matthew 7:7–8

CONTENTS

A Word to Our Readers xi
Foreword..xv
Introduction..xvii

Chapter 1   Our Unique Journeys into Christ Jesus 1
Chapter 2   The Blueprint for Becoming an Optimal Disciple:
            The New Covenant.. 13
Chapter 3   Peter's Path to an Optimal Life 27
Chapter 4   Discerning Your Promise(s): The Gifts from His
            Glory and Goodness 39
Chapter 5   How God Prepared the Soil of Your Soul to
            Become an Optimal Disciple 51
Chapter 6   Key Attitudes and Insights of an Optimal Disciple 61
Chapter 7   How Do the Magnificent and Precious Promises
            Become a Light to Your Path? 78
Chapter 8   The God of Your Promises 88
Chapter 9   Cultivating His Magnificent Promises 117
Chapter 10 The Garden He Designed for You. 135

Epilogue... 145
Discovery Questions 149

A WORD TO OUR READERS

Thank you for choosing this book. Perhaps the title grabbed your attention, and you thought, *Yes, I want to be an optimal disciple of Jesus Christ!* Or maybe it was the subtitle that caught your eye: Discovering How Christ Has Been Discipling You!

Either way, it's safe to assume you have a personal relationship with Jesus and have already entered the kingdom of light through faith in Him. And since Jesus Christ is God incarnate—worthy of our highest devotion, it's only natural to desire more from our walk with Him.

Just as the Holy Spirit led you to Christ in a way that spoke uniquely to your heart, He continues to disciple you personally, shaping your journey with a tailored touch. This book was written with you in mind. Whether you're a new believer just beginning your faith journey or a seasoned follower, the purpose here is to help you recognize how Christ has been personally discipling you all along. By deepening that awareness, you can unlock the abundant life He offers and step fully into your role as His disciple. And as you grow into a more faithful disciple, you will also become a better discipler, equipping others to follow Christ more fully.

Here's who I hope will benefit from these pages:

- Anyone who wants to experience the abundant life Christ offers.
- New believers who desire the closest relationship with Christ possible, uniquely designed for them.
- Long-term followers of Christ whose disciple-making efforts have fallen short of expectations.
- Believers who, after years of following Christ, sense a deeper call to intimacy with Him.
- Anyone looking to optimize their personal plan for spiritual formation.

In the context of this book, the word *optimal* means "the best possible way" for ***you*** to follow Christ and become the disciple and disciple-maker He designed you to be. It's about maximizing your potential and advancing your spiritual growth. I am confident that if you approach this with a humble heart and truly seek to "become partakers of the divine nature," as the apostle Peter describes in 2 Peter 1:4, you will grow into the optimal disciple Christ intends you to be.

Peter provides a clear roadmap for spiritual growth in the verses that follow, urging believers to add to their faith virtues like moral excellence, knowledge, self-control, endurance, godliness, mutual affection, and love (2 Peter 1:5–7). These qualities are similar to the fruit of the Spirit, and they will grow in your life as you intentionally partake of the divine nature. Peter then summarizes in verse 8 by stating, "For if these qualities (of God) are in you and increasing, they keep you from being ineffective and unproductive in the knowledge of our Lord Jesus Christ."

I have personally experienced the truth of this principle in both positive *and* negative ways. When I diligently pursued Christ through the scriptural promises He gave me, my spiritual life flourished. But when I neglected them, my growth withered. However, this book is not about my life—it's about you and how you can become an optimal disciple by applying Peter's teachings.

But there's something even more foundational at work here. As you begin to understand Peter's path, you'll discover that Christ has been discipling you all along. This may be a new realization for some, but it's a key truth: Jesus is not only the One we follow—He is also the One actively shaping us. The more you recognize this ongoing work of Christ in your life, the more effective you will become as both a disciple and disciple-maker. In the chapters ahead, we will explore how the biblical promises He has given you and your intentional cooperation with His guidance through them will cause your love for Jesus to increase and transform your spiritual journey.

Peter's path to discipleship works with *any* biblical discipleship program or spiritual formation ministry, especially if you minister to hurting and broken people. This is not some magic method, but the assurance that whoever humbly follows Peter's path will encounter the divine nature of Christ, becoming transformed and conformed into the image of God's

Son—the optimal destination for all discipleship paths. This book will equip you with practical tools and insights that will not only complement but also enhance your current practices of seeking God.

The optimal path to following Christ is discovered by actively cooperating with the Holy Spirit. This book will help you recognize how God has been instructing, teaching, and guiding you through the new relational covenant Jesus sacrificed to give you. You will discover your unique path through which the Holy Spirit is already discipling and transforming you. Each person God calls into His kingdom is given a unique, personal path to follow (Colossians 2:6–7). Every true believer in God's Living Son has already been equipped for a distinctive journey of following Christ. As you become consistent and intentional about your own path, you can help others find theirs, embracing your unique and valuable role in God's plan. The disciple transforms into the discipler.

This book offers scriptural insight into how the Holy Spirit has been discipling you and how you can actively participate in your journey of following Christ. As a believer in Christ Jesus, you already have some awareness of the personalized promises He has given you.

Since this concept is a key principle in this book, I believe a clear definition is essential for understanding:

Personalized Promise: The personalized messages from God that give us hope and grace as we experience His glory and goodness, enabling us to partake of the divine nature (2 Peter 1:3–4; Psalm 119:49). While the promises in Scripture are universal to all believers, the Holy Spirit uniquely applies these promises to each believer's life. This Spirit-led application makes God's promises personally meaningful, guiding and encouraging each believer according to their specific needs, circumstances, and growth. Rather than creating new promises, the Holy Spirit helps us experience God's timeless truths in ways that deepen our relationship with Him and empower us to live out His purposes and promises as we partake of the divine nature.

Now, this book will help you sharpen that focus and fully embrace the path He has already prepared for you. This path includes inward disciplines like prayer, meditation, solitude, and fasting, which nurture personal spiritual growth, and outward disciplines like service, evangelism, celebration, and stewardship, which enhance your relationship with others. These practices enable you to partake of His power, not your own, as you walk in the fullness of this plan for your life. However, as the cover of this book is adorned with a Lion-knocker to remind us to draw near to God, we need to be willing to "Keep on asking, and it will be given to you. Keep on seeking, and you will find. Keep on knocking and the door will be opened to you. For everyone who asks receives, those who seek find, and the door will be opened to whomever knocks" (Matthew 7:7–8).

Jesus said, "I am the gate" (John 10:9), and there are passages or promises that are like gates designed for you to enter into God's thoughts (Isaiah 55:8–11). Your heavenly Father has already unlocked them through the sacrifice of his Son, Christ Jesus. The Holy Spirit reveals the way, the truth, and the life by which we come to the Father through Him, the Lion of our salvation. Second Peter 1 offers a clear description of this path. Yet, it's essential to remember the importance of walking humbly as you ask, seek, and knock, embracing the promises through the guidance of the Holy Spirit.

His yoke is truly easy, and His burden is light, but only when we walk the path His way (Matthew 11:30).

FOREWORD

When I read a book of theology, there are certain qualities I'm looking for. I want to see that the author is engaging with the Scriptures, and with the deep riches contained within the Christian tradition. I want to see that the author has an understanding of human nature, or at least a desire to connect to readers as human beings, acknowledging that we are creatures made in the image of God who are nevertheless frail and imperfect because of sin. But perhaps most importantly—and this is especially true when the book is about the Christian life, about growing in the way of Jesus—I want to know something about the author's character. I want to know whether the life that the author is living lines up with the words on the page, and if the fruits that the author is bearing in Christian community are helping others to flourish in their faith.

Admittedly, this isn't always possible. While I may be able to research the backgrounds of authors, and hear reports about authors from those who do know them, I don't get the opportunity to see how, or whether, the author is applying to his or her own life the ideas they write about. This book, for me, is different. One of the reasons why I'm so excited about the publication of this book is because I have been blessed to know Neil DeSiato for a number of years, and have seen that the convictions he talks about within these pages aren't just a matter of theoretical musing or interesting speculation. They matter to him. And because they matter to him, he is able to help others see why they might matter to them as well.

This book is a labor of love for Neil. It is borne out of the work that God has been doing in his life, as Neil seeks to understand more fully what it might mean to be a disciple of Jesus. One of the surest signs of maturity is a commitment never to stop learning, a passion never to stop growing. These are commitments and passions that Neil possesses in abundance, along with a desire to help cultivate these commitments and passions in others. When Neil talks about the promises of God in this book, he does so from a place of seeing these promises reach fulfillment and bear fruit in his own life. He can write about these things with such joy because he knows the delight of tasting God's goodness, the joy that comes, even after long decades of walking with God, when we learn something new about our Creator.

This is not a labor confined to the pages of a book. The ways that these realities have been manifest in Neil's life can't be contained within two covers or enumerated by a word count. Over the past several years, I have watched as Neil has introduced these ideas to numerous people in our small community. At men's breakfasts and retreats, Neil and others have opened themselves up to real, authentic conversation about what it might look like to grow in Christ, according to the promises that God has for us, and how we might rediscover the first love that God revealed to us when he called us. In day to day conversations, in coffee shops and on sidewalks, through encouraging texts and in times of prayer, I have watched and listened as Neil has unpacked for numerous people, both men and women, younger and older, from a number of churches and denominational backgrounds, what it might look like to draw near to the God who makes promises and the God who fulfills those promises.

Neil would be the first to say that none of this is because of him. Neil has worked hard, to be sure. Neil is committed and diligent when it comes to sharing what God has revealed to him in ways that might make a difference to others. But he is also quick to acknowledge, as Paul says to the Corinthians, that it is not him working but the grace of God working in him. Neil lives by the conviction that the Holy Spirit works in people's lives, so that when hearts and habits are changed through Neil's words, those words are just the tools used by a good God to accomplish his purposes. It's my hope that this book, likewise, will be a tool that God uses to change people's lives, so that they might understand more fully the journey of discipleship and that they might embrace more fully the promises that God makes, and fulfills, in the lives of his children.

Grace and Peace,
Todd Edmondson, Pastor, First Christian Church, Erwin

INTRODUCTION

The way of the righteous is like the dawning light that shines brighter and brighter until full daylight.

PROVERBS 4:18

Let me introduce myself and share why I wrote this book as I pursued becoming an optimal disciple. This is the story of my journey to live an abundant spiritual life and faithfully follow Jesus Christ as devoted disciple. Along the way, through both my successes and failures, I've gained valuable insights that I believe will encourage and guide you in your own walk with Christ.

I came to faith in Christ in 1970 when I was 19 years old. Prior to that, I believed there was a God, but I struggled to accept that God could become a man; therefore, I chose to be an agnostic whenever it was convenient to sin. Still, I occasionally attended Catholic or Protestant church services, hoping to find a way to stop sinning or do some religious act to be good enough for God's acceptance.

My spiritual change eventually occurred in the only way possible—through God's providence. At one service, I was listening to a preacher named Freddie Gage. His message was not about sin but about God's promise that I could have a relationship with God the Father. He taught that God wanted to be your Father and that you could become adopted into His family by choosing Jesus Christ.

It's an amazing mystery how simple words empowered by the Holy Spirit can open hearts and activate faith in Christ. That's exactly what happened to me. That night, I chose to believe and begin a relationship with Jesus as my Savior and Lord. I went from an agnostic to a believer overnight. My spiritual eyes were open, and the epiphany I received still lives in me today: Jesus Christ is God, come in the flesh! God enabled me to believe what I couldn't in my own strength.

The next day, I experienced a hunger for God's Word and the newfound ability to read it with insight and understanding. I also desired what I normally avoided: fellowship with God's people. I began my spiritual journey, not in an organized church, but in gatherings that met weekly in various homes. My hunger and thirst for knowing Christ was insatiable, so I attended these home Bible studies every night. Soon after, I was baptized in the ocean in Hollywood Beach, Florida. Then, in the fall of 1970, I enrolled in a small interdenominational Bible college in San Antonio, Texas.

Shortly after I began classes, the dean of men told me that I must find a church home—one that the college approved. At that point, I had little faith in organized religion, and I was not happy about being told I had to commit to a structured church. I had never joined or become a member of any church before, so this was an awkward decision. Since I didn't embrace this idea, I waited until I was almost expelled before complying.

I quickly learned that many other behaviors, such as wearing my hair long, also had to go if I wanted to remain in college. But I loved Jesus and believed God had led me to this place. Therefore, I also joyfully sold my 1963 Austin-Healey 3000 to pay my school bills.

My zeal for Christ and sharing the good news was intense, so I spent a lot of time in downtown San Antonio with other students sharing the gospel with anyone who would listen. We would present the gospel, and if the person was willing to place their trust in Christ, we would pray with them right on the spot and lead them into God's presence. One evening, a fellow student and I led twenty-seven men and women into God's kingdom!

I loved the Lord, and leading people to Christ was an intensely joyful experience, yet, sadly, I did not disciple any of those people that first year. I was in classes learning the Bible but was not discipling anyone, and no one was teaching me how to disciple others. While there were courses on how to share the gospel and to lead people into God's kingdom, none provided practical instruction on how to disciple someone or help them understand how Christ was being formed within them. At that point, I sensed Jesus calling me into ministry as a pastor/teacher. I also strongly felt I would someday start and lead a church in San Antonio. However, I had never been "rooted in a local church," meaning deeply connected and committed to a specific church community. So, the idea of being called into pastoral ministry was a dreadful thought. I loved learning and telling others about Christ, but pastoring and leading a church was another thing altogether!

Still, I loved the Lord and began equipping myself to become the minister I believed Jesus wanted me to be. I graduated with a degree in ministry, then went to the University of Texas and earned a Bachelor of Science in Psychology. During that time, I joined a large interdenominational church in San Antonio to gain as much hands-on experience as possible in becoming a pastor and teacher, and to learn the practical aspects of leading a church.

I watched, listened, copied, and modeled what I believed would train me to become a pastor worthy of Christ's calling. I loved my pastor and shared my dream with him of starting a church in San Antonio. He welcomed the idea and allowed me to serve in various areas of the church. In 1973, I was ordained into gospel ministry there. Then, not two years later, my pastor unexpectedly left to establish another church. After a few months, another gifted speaker and minister became the church's new leader. I shared my dream of starting a church with him, and he seemed pleased and asked me to continue serving, even promoting me to assistant pastor. After a few years, I also became an elder. It was then that the pastor started inviting guest speakers to teach about what it means to be a disciple of Jesus Christ.

These teachers taught primarily that discipleship involved obedience to earthly leaders. Each senior pastor of the local church was to be like the "Moses" leader in the congregation—to seek God for the congregation so he could tell each person how they could know and do God's will. It may seem obvious to some of you that this teaching was heretical. But at that time, I did not know the Bible well enough to recognize this error. It appeared valid, given the experience and knowledge of the pastor and the teachers he invited to the pulpit. Lacking clarity about how to make a disciple and knowing my employment meant working with the program, I did not speak up for a while. But eventually I realized that their doctrine was not right.

Soon, other lay leaders also began to sense errors in the teachings on discipleship that conflicted with solid new covenant theology. When I voiced my concerns as an elder, I became a threat to my pastor. Not surprisingly, he soon "discerned" that God's will for me was to leave San Antonio to serve a pastorate in Northern California. I did go and spend a week there. It was a newly established work with a precious group of Christ-loving people. Yet, I knew God had already called me to start a church in San Antonio. When I returned home, I told my pastor I could not go and that I was to start a new church in the city. He became angry, suggesting I was trying to make him look bad. He further suggested I was trying to divide the church. I asked him for nothing more than to be released from my responsibilities there and to be enabled to follow God's calling to start a church in San Antonio.

After consulting with the discipleship teachers, the pastor called me into a meeting with twenty leaders. I was given an ultimatum: repent and submit to the "Moses" of the church or face church discipline. I raised questions about my responsibility to follow the Lord and not violate my conscience, but they dismissed my concerns, insisting that by rejecting the authority of my spiritual "Moses," I was in rebellion. As a result, they excommunicated me from the fellowship.

Not long after, the church held a "Solemn Assembly" with approximately 800 members in attendance. I sat quietly in the back as they publicly denounced me, labeling my actions as "wicked" and warning the congregation that it would be dangerous to follow me or my teachings.

Though I never imagined it would happen under these circumstances, I felt led to finally step into my calling to start a new church at that point. Surprisingly, on the first Sunday, over two hundred people from my previous church attended. It was a difficult and unfortunate time for the church I had left, as there was significant backlash to their heavy-handed approach. Looking back, I know I did not cause division; I simply provided a place of worship for those who wanted to follow Jesus. Still, I wish I had waited a year or more before starting the new church. I never wanted to be part of any division within the body of Christ. I was young and still working out my walk with Christ. Despite my many failings, God's faithfulness never wavered, and He has continued to sustain me in Christ to this day. It probably comes as no surprise that, after that painful experience, I avoided any teaching on discipleship for many years. The wounds from that false, manipulative approach to making disciples and guiding others in spiritual formation left a deep scar. That was my introduction to Practical Discipleship 101, a great lesson in what the Bible does *not* teach about spiritual formation.

Several years later, on Christmas Eve 1997, my wife, Eunice, and I launched another church in San Antonio. By that time, I recognized the need for a deeper understanding of how to encourage spiritual formation in those I pastored. Together with the men and elders, I sought God's guidance on the true process of becoming a disciple and making disciples. I read books by successful disciple-makers and turned to godly leaders, asking key questions: How are disciples made? How can I become an effective disciple-maker?

The fog began to lift when I read Gary Thomas' book *Sacred Marriage*. It helped me grasp the humility required to truly love my wife by learning to cooperate with God's Spirit, allowing Him to love her through me. Another breakthrough came as I asked, "Lord, how have you discipled me?" "What was I doing when my passion for Christ increased, and my humility towards God and others grew deeper?" This book is the result of seeking God, meditating on His Word, listening to godly leaders, and recognizing how the Holy Spirit kept and sustained me in Christ for over 50 years. Now, I not only embrace Jesus' command to His church to make disciples (Matthew 28); I also understand, through the lens of 2 Peter 1, how God uniquely disciples each one of us.

Let me share a brief summary of my transformation. By God's grace, I experienced a profound change overnight. I transitioned from being a lost soul, far from faith in Jesus Christ, to a believer with confidence in Him for over 50 years. The night I prayed, marked a pivotal moment, one that forever changed the course of my life. My journey from spiritual darkness into the light of knowing God began with a simple prayer, but that was just the start. It opened the door to discovering God's immense and profound plan to shape me into the image of His Son.

I am certain that your journey to faith in Jesus Christ was just as unique. Each of us enters the kingdom of God in different ways, all empowered by faith. How we came to that faith is often a mystery. Jesus alluded to this when he spoke with Nicodemus in John chapter 3. While this passage is often studied to explain how a person enters God's kingdom, it also offers tremendous insights into how we can cooperate with the Holy Spirit as He disciples us into becoming optimal followers of Christ.

CHAPTER 1

OUR UNIQUE JOURNEYS INTO CHRIST JESUS

I am not ashamed of the gospel, because it is the instrument of God's power that brings salvation for everyone who believes.
ROMANS 1:16

Discipleship is the process of becoming a committed follower of Jesus Christ, aligning our lives more closely with His teachings and example. It's not just about learning doctrine but involves a transformative journey that reshapes our character, priorities, and actions. As disciples, we're called to grow in our love for God and others, reflecting Christ's love in how we live, serve, and share the gospel. The desire to become better disciples springs from the understanding that our lives are meant to glorify God, mirror Christ, and bear witness to His grace and truth in a world that deeply needs Him.

Traditional approaches to discipleship in the church have often centered on formal teachings, classes, and programs that convey biblical knowledge and moral guidance. While these methods have value, they can fall short of producing deeply transformed disciples. Research has established that 39 percent of all Christians are not engaged in discipleship at all. And just one-third of Christians (33 percent) are disciple-makers, actively helping someone grow in faith and move closer to Christ. Overall, that leaves about two in five Christians lacking any kind of discipleship.

This is where the Spirit-led application of God's promises becomes invaluable. Unlike traditional discipleship methods, which often rely on structured teachings and programs, a Spirit-led approach starts with the awareness that, "He who began a good work in you will bring it to completion" (Philippians 1:6). Christ's Spirit is our personal guide, tailoring each believer's journey to resonate deeply with their unique creation and God's plan and purpose for their lives. This personalized discipleship not only nurtures a stronger relationship with God but also empowers us to live out His promises with genuine transformation. As a result, Spirit-led discipleship fosters growth that goes beyond having biblical knowledge as mere academic knowledge to knowing Christ deeply and personally. This encourages believers to walk confidently in their identity in Christ and become effective disciple-makers themselves.

Where It All Begins

Our journey towards becoming optimal disciples begins with our understanding of how God first welcomes us into His kingdom. God invites us to follow Christ by believing in the gospel, God's good news. Yet, many people remain unaware of what the gospel truly is. The apostle Paul presents it clearly in 1 Corinthians 15:1–4:

> *Now, brothers and sisters, I make known to you the gospel, which I preached to you, which you received, on which you have taken your stand, and by which you are saved, if you hold firmly to the word I preached to you. Otherwise, you have believed in vain. For I delivered to you as most important what I received: that Christ died for our sins according to the Scriptures. He was buried; he was raised on the third day according to the Scriptures.*

After the resurrection, this message was proclaimed by the apostles throughout the book of Acts and is to be declared by God's messengers today.

Before Jesus was crucified, buried, and rose from the dead, He revealed how the gospel would impact the human heart to a religious leader named Nicodemus in John 3:1–15. Jesus used the powerful metaphor of being born again, representing a spiritual rebirth—a transformation of the heart and mind. The joy of experiencing a family member's birth or being part of creating a new life is a familiar experience for many, making this metaphor deeply relatable. Jesus tells Nicodemus, "Unless a person is born again, they cannot see the kingdom of God" (John 3:3). This spiritual rebirth is a fundamental concept in Christianity, signifying a new life in Christ.

Spiritual Formation Is as Mysterious as the Movement of the Wind

Nicodemus was a Pharisee, a member of a Jewish religious sect known for its strict adherence to the Scriptures and their commands. He was also a respected Jewish leader, whom Jesus referred to as "a teacher of Israel," signifying his reputation as a scholar and a renowned Rabbi. Nicodemus came to Jesus because he recognized that Jesus was a teacher sent from God.

As we reflect on this encounter, let us put ourselves in Nicodemus' place as someone who earnestly believes God's Word, takes it seriously, and seeks Jesus for deeper understanding of how spiritual transformation occurs:

> *Now a Pharisee named Nicodemus, a Jewish leader, came to Jesus at night and said, "Rabbi, we know that you are a teacher who has come from God, for no one could perform the miracles that you do unless God is with him." Jesus replied, "I'm telling you the truth: Unless a person is born again, they cannot see the kingdom of God." Nicodemus replied, "How can a person be born when they're old? Surely, they cannot enter their mother's womb a second time to be born again!' Jesus replied, "I'm telling you the truth: Unless one is born of both water and the Spirit, they cannot enter the kingdom of God. What is born from the flesh is flesh, and what is born from the Spirit is spirit. So don't be amazed that I told you, 'You must be born again.' The wind blows wherever it pleases, and you hear the sound of it, but you cannot tell where it comes from or where it is going. So it is with everyone who is born of the Spirit"* (John 3:1–8).

Jesus' conversation with Nicodemus reveals the critical truth, that we must be "born again" to enter the kingdom of God, and that this new birth involves being "born of both water and the Spirit." As Nicodemus struggles to understand, Jesus responds with these words:

> *Nicodemus asked, "How can these things be?" "You're a teacher of Israel," Jesus replied, "and you don't understand these things? I'm telling you the truth: We speak about what we know, and we testify about what we've seen, but you people still don't accept our testimony. If I have told you about earthly things and you do not believe, how will you believe if I speak of heavenly things? No one has ever ascended into heaven except the one who descended from heaven, the Son of Man. Just as Moses lifted up the snake in the wilderness, the Son of Man must be lifted up so that everyone who believes in him may have eternal life"* (John 3:9–15).

In this passage, Jesus clarifies what it means to be born again and confirms that everyone who believes in Him may have eternal life. To illustrate this, He refers to a well-known story from the Old Testament (Numbers 21:8–9), when Moses led the nation of Israel through the wilderness.

During their journey, the Israelites became dissatisfied, grumbled, and rebelled against both Moses' leadership and God. In response, God sent venomous snakes among them. When the people repented, God instructed Moses to make a bronze snake and lift it up, telling the people that anyone who looked at it in faith would be healed. This metaphor illustrates how simple faith in God's promises can "save" us from the venomous poison of our sins. It only took a "look" with faith that made the difference for the Israelites. Just as they were healed by looking at the bronze snake, so we too can receive salvation through a single act of faith in Jesus.

The apostle Paul writes in 2 Corinthians 5:21, "God made Jesus, the one who had no sin, to be the sin offering for us so that in him we might become the righteousness of God." The snake, being a symbol of evil and sin, was lifted in the same way Jesus was lifted on the cross as He took our sin and evil upon Himself. He became the sacrifice for our sin, and we received His righteousness. This salvation is what God offers to everyone who believes in the gospel of the kingdom of God. Yet, it is imperative to know that the mystery of our coming to Christ and receiving His righteousness is as controllable as the wind. In other words, the epiphany of our faith in Christ is not controllable—at least not by us. It is a very personal, unique experience with Christ that each born-again believer experiences. The revelation of Jesus Christ to you, when you *first* believed and trusted Jesus as your Savior and Lord, is only the beginning of your journey with Christ.

As I related earlier, my personal experience was an almost instantaneous spiritual transformation. At age 19, I changed from a pagan to a zealous follower of Jesus Christ. However, my wife's experience was quite different. Her path to Christ started very young, as she grew up in a family that attended a Lutheran church. I expect your entrance into the kingdom of God may be somewhere in-between ours.

To explain the mystery of how each person comes to their epiphany of faith in Jesus Christ and "born again" is not only impossible but fruitless—like trying to catch the wind. The main point is that we must personally know that *the wind has caught us*. Recognizing that our entrance into the God's kingdom is guided uniquely by His Spirit highlights the importance of appreciating God's personal relationship with each of us. This uniqueness individually reflects how God *has been* discipling you, *is currently* discipling you, and *will continue* to disciple you throughout your spiritual journey (Philippians 1:6). No one is exactly like you, which means your transformation into the likeness of God's Son will be uniquely yours as well.

So, what's your story of coming to Christ? How did you begin to see and desire to enter the kingdom of God and receive His eternal life? What made you recognize that Jesus Christ is God in the flesh? While I may not know the details of how you received everlasting life by trusting in Jesus, whatever way you came into the kingdom, gave birth to your original confidence. That confident faith, through knowing Jesus Christ is your conviction of the truth, reflecting what Jesus prays in John 17:3, "Now this is eternal life: that they know you, the only true God, and Jesus Christ, whom you have sent."

What was the word, message, or epiphany God gave you that inspired you to place your faith in the Risen Christ? The psalmist says, "Remember your word to your servant, in which you have made me hope" (Psalm

119:49). That revelation was a message of *hope*, your personal epiphany of Jesus Christ, and the beginning of your life in Him.

Your Unique Journey Comes from a Unique Relationship

Jesus' life, death, and resurrection established a new relationship between God and humanity. By trusting in Him, we are transferred into God's eternal life, where He reigns as King—this is the kingdom of God. All who believe in the gospel enter this kingdom and receive eternal life. As believers, we live under the promises that reveal the *new reality* prophesied by Jeremiah and Ezekiel: the new covenant, forged by Jesus' through His obedience to the Father in dying for our sins. Christ instituted this new covenant during the Last Supper.

The following promises were spoken through God's prophets and explain the new covenant:

- You will know God personally (Jeremiah 31:34).
- God will reveal Himself to you as your Father, and you will be His child (1 John 3:1).
- God will forgive all your rebellion and sin (Jeremiah 31:34).
- The Spirit of God will dwell in you (Ezekiel 36:27).
- God will guide you and teach you His ways (Isaiah 30:21).
- God will give you a new heart that loves Him and desires to obey His will (Ezekiel 36:26).
- You will receive all this and "everything we need pertaining to life and godliness" (2 Peter 1:3) when you trust in Jesus Christ.

This truth is a unilateral sovereign work of God in us—the salvation we have received through Christ. This is the inheritance of all who are in Christ and have received His righteousness by faith.

After receiving this eternal life and the new promises from God, you are also given a new identity, mission, and purpose for living. Before ascending into heaven, Jesus Christ entrusted His followers with this mission, known as the Great Commission. This is the divine mandate and purpose for every believer, as well as for His church throughout all generations. Jesus commands us in Matthew 28:19–20, "Go therefore and make disciples of all nations, baptizing them in the name of the Father and of the Son, and of the Holy Spirit, teaching them to observe everything that I have commanded you. And look, I am with you always, to the end of the age."

How you are to go and fulfill your purpose is revealed in Colossians 2:6–7, "Therefore walk in Christ Jesus the Lord, just as you have received Him and just as you were taught, firmly rooted, built up in Him, established in the faith, and overflowing with thanksgiving." You are to walk, which means to live out your faith, just as you have received Him. Receiving Christ, believing Christ, or coming to faith, however you describe it, was a unique experience. How you "walk" or follow Christ to make disciples will also be a unique experience between you and your heavenly Father.

Your Mission to Baptize and Teach

The two significant aspects of your new mission are *baptism* and *teaching*. These two actions describe not only how you are to walk but also what you are called to do as a new believer.

Baptism reveals humility, the essential attitude of your heart towards God and others. Jesus commanded baptism as evidence of submission to God, designed to acknowledge and produce humility in the hearts of His followers. Baptism, a symbol of our faith, has the transformative power to humble us and lead us on the path of righteousness. A disciple of Jesus Christ must understand that God gives grace only to the humble, and it is through this grace-filled humility that we are transformed into the image of His Son. Human effort and self-centered pride cannot produce Christ's humility within us. Therefore, it is our reverence for Jesus Christ that reveals the basic humility required to begin and sustain our life in him.

Jesus' response to His disciple Thomas gives us insight into the central role Christ plays in our relationship with God the Father. When Thomas seeks understanding of how to go to God, Jesus declares, "I am the way and the truth and the life. No one comes to the Father except through me" (John 14:6), revealing that He is the only path to God. Walking in that way, believing that truth, and entering that life are only possible through repentance—turning away from unbelief and the ways of the world—and fully submitting to God through His Son.

1 Our Unique Journeys

Jesus Christ, the Son of God, demonstrated the power of godly humility by coming into the world through the womb of the Virgin Mary. The apostle Paul writes, "He [Jesus] emptied himself, taking the very nature of a servant, being made in human likeness, and being found in appearance as a man; he humbled himself by becoming obedient to death—even death on a cross!" (Philippians 2:7–8).

The apostle further describes the connection between our baptism and the humility of dying to self: "Don't you know that all of us who have been baptized into Christ Jesus have been baptized into his death? Therefore we were buried with him through baptism into death, *(symbolizing our death to sin and self)* so we too may walk in a new life, just as Christ was raised from the dead through the glory of the Father" (Romans 6:3–4, emphasis mine).

Baptism is the first part of the Great Commission because it teaches us to recognize humility towards God as an essential aspect of our new identity and relationship with Him. Through humble faith, we received Christ as our Savior, which is how we now walk with Him. As an optimal disciple, we continue to live out the humble repentance of our baptism, recognizing we've been crucified with Christ and are dependent on Him.

The attitude of an optimal disciple would be like that of the apostle Paul, "I have been crucified with Christ. I no longer live, but Christ lives in me. The life I now live in the body, I live by faith in the Son of God, who loved me and gave himself up for me" (Galatians 2:20). Living by "faith in the Son of God" is made possible through the power of the indwelling Holy Spirit, whom God has given to every believer as part of the new covenant promises. The more you allow the Holy Spirit to live and love through you in genuine humility towards God and others, the more you can convey the truth of who Jesus Christ is to others. The Holy Spirit is the only one who can empower us to live a life of humility and love towards Jesus Christ, therefore enabling us to reflect the character of Christ to the world.

The second major part of Jesus' Great Commission command is "teaching them to observe everything that I have commanded you" (Matthew 28:20). The most important teaching we can share with others is the personal, living instructions, promises, and convictions between God the Father and ourselves, showing how He has loved us. Jesus gave this command to His disciples on His last night with them, "Love one another as I have loved you" (John15:12). This teaching goes beyond moral rules, intellectual assent, or theological doctrines. It's more than simply learning to be a "good" church attendee. It also doesn't stop at knowing and teaching the great doctrinal truths of the Christian faith.

The most important commands Jesus teaches you are the personal, living instructions of how God loves you and how you are to love others, including the promises given to you by your Father in heaven. The greatest promises you receive are the revelation of who God is and who you are in Him—your new identity in Christ. They are the words of truth that continually stir faith, hope, and love in your heart. Through these instructions and personal convictions, you manifest what it means to love the Lord with all your heart, mind, soul, and strength, and to love others as you love yourself (Matthew 22:37–39).

The purpose of His commands is to reveal God the Father, His truths, His ways, and His eternal life. While solid biblical doctrine is essential, its primary purpose is to help you manifest Jesus Christ to the world, showing how He has loved you. Therefore, the entire process of following Christ must be deeply personal, humble, intentional, and all-consuming in your heart. No one can live this spiritual life through human strength or pride; it must be powered by the Holy Spirit through humble communion with Christ and His Word in an intimate spiritual relationship.

This is the kind of relationship God offers and desires to have with you. He calls you to seek Him with your whole heart, not to *become* qualified for heaven, for only He can qualify you with His righteousness, but because, as a believer, you are already included in His covenant of faith and called His own. You are His instrument of love and change in this world.

Your Journey Is Very Personal

As you seek God through the promises He's given you, you will cooperate with the Holy Spirit and discover your optimal spiritual life. Paul states it clearly in Philippians 2:12–13, "Therefore, my beloved, just as you have always obeyed (not only in my presence but now much more in my absence), work out your salvation with fear and trembling, for it is God who works in you to will and to work for his good pleasure." As an optimal disciple, you will be motivated by grace to *continually* "work out" the salvation you have received, knowing it is God's power working through you. You may respond, "Only Jesus Christ did that!" That's true, but remember, you are made in God's image and being conformed and transformed into the image of His Son. So, as Christ lives through you, you will experience His grace to do His will.

What did you receive when you accepted salvation from God? Take a moment to reflect on Romans 12:1–2, "Therefore I urge you, brothers and sisters, in view of the merciful acts of God, offer your bodies as a living sacrifice, holy and pleasing to God, which is your reasonable worship. Don't be conformed to the pattern of this age; rather, be transformed by the renewing of your mind so that you'll prove what God's will is—the good, pleasing, and perfect will of God."

The "therefore" in Romans 12:1 points back to the previous eleven chapters of Paul's letter to the early church in Rome, where he explains in great detail the wondrous ways God has "worked" His salvation into you through His "merciful acts." These merciful acts are the ways He reveals Christ's glory and excellence to give you His "magnificent and precious promises" (2 Peter 1:4).

Christ's promises to you are *his perfectly chosen words or messages*, revealed through "the merciful acts of God" as you experience Jesus' glory. These merciful acts are not abstract or theoretical facts of what God did somewhere to someone. They are the ways the One, "who called [you] by his own glory and excellence" (2 Peter 1:3), has revealed Himself to you and given you His magnificent promises. What acts of mercy have you experienced, and how have they transformed you?

God works through the promises He has given you to *conform and transform* you into the image of Christ. These truths are specifically designed for each of His children, enabling us to become mature followers of Christ who manifest God's good, acceptable, and perfect will. In 2 Peter 1, we see the pathway God has been guiding you on, leading you to cooperate with His Spirit to be fruitful and fulfill His plan for your life. The Holy Spirit seeks to teach you how to partake of God's divine nature therefore, producing His qualities in your life. Through Christ in you, the power of God's Spirit will flow through you, empowering you to overcome iniquity in your life. This promise of transformation is a beacon of hope, encouraging you in your spiritual journey.

Therefore, you must follow the path and ways God has *revealed to you*, allowing Him to live in you and love through you for His glory. His command to "go and make disciples" is not a directive to simply convert a person, but to teach them by your behavior and words what it means to love the Lord with all their heart, soul, mind, and body. Making disciples clearly defines your purpose. As a follower of Jesus Christ, you are called to embrace both aspects of His command: *to walk humbly with God and to love others as He loves you* (Micah 6:8; John 13:34) .

Therefore, as an optimal disciple, you are called to hold fast to the promises God gave you when Christ first called you to Himself through His glory and goodness (2 Peter 1:3-4). These promises reveal God's first love for you. As an optimal disciple, your mission is to continually cultivate the love and grace you received when God first opened your spiritual eyes. By believing and engrafting God's promises into your heart, your life will be filled with purpose and passion for Christ and His will. This passion is empowered by your ongoing journey to become "partakers of *(and participants in)* the divine nature" of God (2 Peter 1:4, addition mine).

This book is designed as a discovery guide to help Christ-followers become more intentional in their obedience to God. It aims to help you "see" with eyes of faith the abundant resources your heavenly Father has provided for you to become both an optimal disciple and disciple-maker.

Understanding Is Essential for Faithfulness

My prayer is that we come to fully grasp the greatness of our inheritance in the kingdom of God, received through the new covenant. When we do, we will become fruitful like the "good" soil in the Parable of the Sower from Matthew 13:23. In this parable, the seed sown on good soil represents the person who "both hears the word and understands it, thus bearing fruit—producing a hundred, sixty, or thirty times what was sown." According to Jesus, the key difference in this fruitful soil—the person's heart—is the word "understands." To understand means to take something apart and put it back together. In the same way, God's promises and His Word must be embraced, lived out, and "taken apart" so they can be rebuilt into our lives. That is the journey I invite you to begin with me.

This book will help you become more aware of how God uniquely saved you and began *uniquely* transforming you into the image of His Son. My hope is that you will begin to discern how Christ, by His Spirit, *has been disciplining you* to become a unique, vibrant follower of Jesus Christ. The more you appreciate *how* you were drawn to Christ and the kingdom of God through His personalized promises to you, the more you begin to cooperate with the Holy Spirit and embrace your identity in Christ. I am thankful you have begun this journey, choosing to allow Christ to reveal His deep and profound love for you.

I pray that God opens your eyes to the hope He has given you in Christ and teaches you to trust the indwelling Holy Spirit. My heartfelt prayer is that you, dear reader, become all that God has designed you to be: His faithful disciple and a grace-filled disciple-maker.

In the next chapter, we'll explore how the new covenant serves as a blueprint, offering insight into how we can begin to cooperate with the Holy Spirit's building plans to shape us into optimal, fruitful, and effective disciples in God's kingdom.

CHAPTER 2

The Blueprint for Becoming an Optimal Disciple: The New Covenant

"Therefore [Jesus Christ] is the mediator of a new covenant, that those who are called may receive the promised eternal inheritance, since a death has occurred as a ransom to redeem them from the penalty of sins committed under the first covenant."

HEBREWS 9:15

We are living in the most gracious period in history since the fall of Adam. By this, I mean that from the time of Christ's coming—through His death, burial, and resurrection—and the sending of the Holy Spirit to dwell within us, our relationship with God has become the most personal it has ever been in all of biblical history. I know this may sound incredible to modern ears, yet when we view it through the lens of God's covenants—His agreements or partnerships with humanity—this final covenant, established through Jesus Christ's, stands out as the most personal and gracious of all.

Throughout biblical history, God established many covenants, each one revealing His promises and faithful loving-kindness towards us. Consider the Noahic Covenant in Genesis 9:11: "I confirm my covenant with you: Never again will all living creatures be drowned by the waters of a flood. Never again will there be a flood to destroy the earth." Now, every rainbow reminds us of God's faithful promise to us, as it did to Noah. Later, God promised King David that he would establish his throne forever through one of David's descendants. Jesus Christ, a descendant of David, fulfilled this enduring promise.

We live within the new covenant, the final covenant established by King Jesus—a partnership more gracious than any God has ever offered humankind. Through this covenant, we're invited into the most personal relationship with God since He walked with Adam in the garden. Unlike previous covenants, God now promises to dwell within us and live through us. He offers us His eternal life, allowing us to live in His reality: He is in us, and we are in Him. Jesus prayed for us to receive this spiritual reality of union with God. In John 17:20–26, Jesus prays that all who believe in Him "may be one, just as you, Father, are in me and I am in you—that they may also be in us so that the world may believe that you have sent me."

A person's relationship with God in the Old Testament is never described as "in Christ." Yet, the apostle Paul often uses this term to explain our new relationship with God. Being in Christ is being in the kingdom of God. The door to the kingdom opens through faith in Christ Jesus, as clearly seen in John 14:6, "I am the way and the truth and the life. No one comes to the Father except through me." You cannot be "in Christ" and not in God's kingdom. All who trust in Jesus enter into the new covenant, receiving a new identity and relationship with God.

To optimize our relationship with the Lord Jesus Christ, we must live in *the reality of* how God relates to us and wants to relate to others through us. Understanding the promises of the new covenant gives us insight into how God has already begun working in all "who have received a faith of the same kind as ours through the righteousness of our God and Savior Jesus Christ" (2 Peter 1:1). Long before the new covenant was instituted at the Last Supper and forged through Jesus Christ's death, burial, and resurrection, it was foretold through the prophets Jeremiah and Ezekiel.

The New Covenant Prophecies—the Blueprint of Our New Life in God

When the prophet Jeremiah foretold the coming of the new covenant, he could not have fully grasped its transformative impact on humanity. The new covenant laid out God's complete design (blueprint) for us, accomplished through the life, death, burial, and resurrection of Jesus

Christ. Its promises form the foundation of how we experience the reality of God's kingdom today.

Blueprints Always Precede Building

I have had the joy of designing and building two houses. In both cases, I sat with a designer, bringing my family's dreams, plans, and ideas to life as the designer created the blueprints. Those blueprints then became our guide to building our dream home with purpose and precision. Similarly, when God the Father designed His final dwelling place on Earth, it wasn't a temple made by human hands. His temple, His dwelling place on Earth, is found within the church—the body of Christ. As Paul writes in Ephesians 2:19–22:

> *So then, you are no longer foreigners and noncitizens but fellow citizens with the saints and members of the household of God, the church, built on the foundation of the apostles and prophets, with Christ Jesus himself as the cornerstone—in whom the whole building, being fitted together, grows into a holy temple in the Lord; in whom you too are being built together into a dwelling place of God (through the Spirit).*

The new covenant prophecies of Jeremiah and Ezekiel have become present promises, serving as "blueprint" promises. When believed and trusted through faith in Jesus Christ, these promises form the foundational support of the church, now God's dwelling place. Through the new covenant, He dwells within each of us and, therefore, within His church.

Just as a blueprint guides the construction of a building, the new covenant, with its transformative promises, guides the spiritual growth of each follower of Jesus Christ. When faithfully believed, this covenant has the power to build us up, making us significant parts of God's dwelling place in this world.

The new covenant provides promises that reveal how believers in Christ are to relate to God, themselves, and others. Through this covenant, each person's transcendent value—surpassing the ordinary and beyond human understanding—is revealed as we realize we are known and loved by God as His children. If I possess this transcendent value because God created me and knows me, then others also hold this same divine worth. This understanding transforms my interactions, allowing me to see others through God's love and His design. Additionally, as a believer, I now have the Spirit of God dwelling *within*, empowering me to love others as He loves me. Jesus Christ made this possible by dying for our sins, forever breaking sin's authority to separate us from God.

When we explore these amazing prophecies and promises found in Hebrews 8, we will discover how Jesus Christ fulfilled God's plan to establish the new covenant as a foundational blueprint, transforming each believer into part of His new community—the church.

The New Covenant Promises

Jeremiah 31:31–34

The author of Hebrews clarifies the promise of the new covenant, quoting directly from Jeremiah 31:31–34 to explain how it differs from the old covenant:

> *But now Jesus, as the mediator of a better covenant, of one established on better promises, has obtained a ministry far superior to the old priesthood. If there had been nothing wrong with the first covenant, no place would have been sought for the second. But when God found fault with the people, he said, "Look! The days are coming, declares the Lord, when I will establish a new covenant with the house of Israel and with the house of Judah. It will not be like the covenant I made with their ancestors at the time when I took them by the hand to lead them out of the land of Egypt, because they did not continue living within my covenant, and I turned away from them, declares the Lord. For this is the covenant I will establish with the house of Israel after those days, declares the Lord. I will put my laws in their minds and write them on their hearts. I will be their God, and they will be my people. Each person will no longer teach their neighbor or say to their brother or sister, 'Know the Lord,' because they*

will all know me, from the least of them to the greatest. For I will forgive their wrongdoing and remember their sins no more" (Hebrews 8:6–12).

The new covenant replaced the old covenant because the old, or Mosaic, covenant did not produce a people who "continue[d]" to obey God (Hebrews 8:9). The old covenant rituals and laws impacted only the external aspects of life, relying of faith but lacking the indwelling Spirit. By contrast, the new covenant, established by Jesus Christ, is empowered by the Spirit of God working within and through those *who believe* its *promises*.

Ezekiel 11:19–20

The prophet Ezekiel also foretold the coming of the new covenant. Through Ezekiel, the Lord promises to transform people's hearts by giving His Spirit to everyone who trusts in Jesus Christ: "I will give them unity, put a new spirit in them, remove the heart of stone from their bodies, and give them a heart of flesh so that they may walk according to my statutes, observe my ordinances, and do them. They will be my people, and I will be their God" (Ezekiel 11:19–20).

God declares in this passage that we will experience an internal change—our hard, sinful hearts will be transformed into soft, obedient hearts. Under the new covenant, a believer receives a transformed heart that longs to do God's will and follow God's ways.

Has this been your experience in Christ since you first believed? I'm not asking if you've led a perfect or sinless life, but rather, do you trust in His promises and genuinely desire to do God's will? Do you keep His commandments out of love for Him? If this isn't your experience, it may be that you haven't yet embraced the fullness of the new covenant reality, allowing the Holy Spirit to transform your mind and lead you to walk in God's ways. You may have faith in Jesus Christ, believe in the gospel, and be assured of your heavenly destination, but still sense you're missing the abundant life that God's new covenant provides.

The gospel is more than just a plan to get people into heaven; it is the power to bring the kingdom of God to Earth. God designed you to receive

2 The Blueprint

Christ's Spirit so that He could live through you, transforming and shaping you to be His co-worker in the world.

The apostle Paul was keenly aware that, despite God's plan, believers don't always live in the way God desires. Consider his words in 1 Corinthians 3:1–4:

> *As for me, brothers and sisters, when I was with you, I could not speak to you as spiritual people, but as worldly people—infants in Christ. I gave you milk, not solid food, for you were not yet ready to receive it. In fact, you are still not ready, for you are still worldly people. As long as there is jealousy and quarreling among you, are you not worldly and living according to the standard of nonbelieving people? For when someone says, "I belong to Paul," and another, "I belong to Apollos," are you not acting like mere humans?*

But God intends for His children not to live "like mere humans"! He offers you an abundant, grace-filled life, inviting you to confidently live in the reality of His new covenant promises. God's plan is for you to grow to be like His Son by learning to partake of His divine nature through the promises of His Word, which He has already given you.

These prophetic truths empower you to understand how God desires you to think about Him, yourself, and others through the grace of Jesus Christ. They are *"being"* or *"identity"* promises, not *"doing"* promises. In other words, they define your new identity and the new life God gave you when you first believed in Jesus Christ. As you *internalize* and embrace these promises by faith, you will be empowered to live differently. Experiencing this new life, as revealed through His promises, will shape you into an optimal disciple of Jesus Christ.

As a believer in the new covenant, you have a unique relationship with God, one defined by His promises. The seven promises declared through the prophets Jeremiah and Ezekiel reveal that everyone who trusts Jesus Christ as their Savior *now has access to this new reality*. These prophecies describe how God now relates to each believer, building on the foundation of Jesus Christ's revelation of God. We have the choice to build our lives with "wood, hay, and stubble" or with "gold, silver, and precious stones"

(1 Corinthians 3:12–13))—a reminder that our own best efforts will fall short, while faith in God's precious promises will produce lasting, eternal value.

The Seven Foundational Promises of The New Covenant

Let's take a closer look at what God promises to everyone who trusts in the finished work of Jesus Christ:

1. "I will put my laws in their minds and write them on their hearts" (Hebrews 8:10).

- You are promised an understanding of God's holy laws and ways within you. By entering the new covenant through faith in Jesus, you come to *know the truth* that sets you free to love God.
- You gain a new motivation because your soul's deepest parts are given a new identity.
- Notice His laws are written not only in your mind but also deeply within your heart. As the psalmist writes in Psalm 51:6, "I see you desire truth in the innermost being; and you teach me wisdom there."

The heart is your innermost being. Psalm 51:6 reveals that God teaches us wisdom there because it's where He establishes our destiny, purpose, identity, and reason for being. God infuses truth into your innermost being so that you may live out the new life He has given you with His wisdom and power. As you trust in Christ, His laws become rooted in your heart; and as you live out this truth, you grow in wisdom.

2. "I will be their God, and they will be my people" (Hebrews 8:10).

- Through Christ's merit, you are adopted into God's family. Though physically born as a descendant of Adam, through faith in Jesus

Christ, you are born again into the Father's family, becoming a true child of God.
- As His child, you have a new inheritance and can forever claim Him as your Father.

3. "Each person will no longer teach their neighbor or say to their brother or sister, 'Know the Lord,' because they will all know me" (Hebrews 8:11).

- Each true believer experiences a revelation of knowing God and the Lord Jesus Christ through a spiritual, internal knowledge given by God.
- This promise assures that when you believe, you receive a personal knowledge of God and Jesus Christ. This knowledge goes beyond intellectual agreement with doctrine; it is a deep knowing that arises from a special relationship born of God's Spirit dwelling within us (John 3:1–8).

4. "From the least of them to the greatest" (Hebrews 8:11).

- This promised relationship is available to *all people* who trust Jesus Christ. Under the old covenant instituted by Moses, only a few—typically the prophet, priest, and king—were anointed by the Holy Spirit and regularly experienced His presence. The Spirit would come upon them for specific purposes, but did not dwell in them permanently.
- When you trust in Jesus Christ, however, you receive God's Holy Spirit to live within you. On the night before His crucifixion, Jesus explained that His departure would ultimately benefit His followers, as He would send the Holy Spirit to be with them forever. In John 14:16–17, Jesus promises, "I will ask the Father, and he will give you another helper to be with you forever—the Spirit of truth—whom the world is not able to receive, because it neither sees him nor knows him. But you do know him, for he remains with you and will be in you" (John 14:16-17).
- Under the old covenant, God's dwelling place was typically the tabernacle or the temple in Israel, and He anointed specific leaders

to fulfill His will. Now, under the new covenant, God promises that His Holy Spirit lives, dwells, and ministers through His people. You are now the dwelling place of God on Earth. We are in Christ, and Christ is in us!

God No Longer Counts Believers' Sins Against Them

5. "For I will forgive their wrongdoing and remember their sins no more" (Hebrews 8:12).

- This gracious promise enables all the above promises to be realized and manifested.
- Through the death, burial, resurrection, and ascension of Jesus Christ to God's throne, God promises us that sin no longer separates believers from Him. As Scripture declares, nothing "will be able to separate us from the love of God that is in Christ Jesus our Lord" (Romans 8:39).
- "All this is from God, who reconciled us to himself through Christ and gave us the ministry of reconciliation: telling others that God was in Christ reconciling the world to himself and not counting people's sins against them" (2 Corinthians 5:18–19).
- The new covenant empowers believers with all its blessings and promises, inviting us to enjoy and live out these truths in the world. "For all the promises of God are 'Yes' (*i.e., fulfilled*) in him. Therefore through him we speak 'Amen' (*i.e., 'so be it'*) to the glory of God" (2 Corinthians 1:20). When we embrace this empowerment, we align ourselves with His Spirit and revelation, speaking the "Amen" over His revealed truth. This act of faith releases the Holy Spirit to live and love through us.

6. "I will give them unity, put a new spirit in them, remove the heart of stone from their bodies, and give them a heart of flesh" (Ezekiel 11:19).

- When we first believed in Jesus Christ, God gave us a new heart, making us a new creation. Just as He promised, he replaces our harden-ed hearts with hearts softened towards Him. With this

new heart, we find freedom from past shame and guilt, allowing us to respond to God's love.
- As believers, we are transformed by this new heart that desires God and His ways. "So then, you can see that if anyone is in Christ, they are a new creation. The old has passed away. Look, the new has come!" 2 Corinthians 5:17.

7. "So that they may walk according to my statutes, observe my ordinances, and do them. They will be my people, and I will be their God" (Ezekiel 11:20).

- When you trusted Christ, you received a heart that desires to follow His statutes and ordinances. Embrace this truth and walk in it.
- As you believe Jesus Christ is God, you are empowered to follow the voice of your Shepherd.
- This promise is available to all who believe, enabling you to reflect that you are His child, created to glorify Him.

In summary, the new covenant, prophesied by the Word of the Lord and instituted through the death, burial, and resurrection of Jesus Christ, allows you to enter into a new identity and reality in God. Until Jesus made the ultimate sacrifice and sent His Holy Spirit, God had never related to humankind as outlined in these prophecies. Through the Son, by the Holy Spirit, you now have an open door to a personal relationship with the living God, enabling you to relate to God from His reality, not yours. He declares that when you believe in Jesus Christ, His moral laws are written in your heart, you are chosen by Him, and you know Him personally. Furthermore, the Holy Spirit is no longer limited to an elite few; He promises to dwell in all who trust in the Lord Jesus Christ. With your sins forgiven at the cross, He has given you a new heart that can and will follow His Spirit.

All of this is yours by His divine power, manifested through you as you live by faith in His promises. This new covenant should give you deep confidence in His commitment to live within you and to complete all He has begun in your life.

We Must Learn to Read the Blueprint.

When the designer handed me the blueprints for my new home, I still needed guidance to understand how to read them and where to begin building.

In the same way, you need to seek the Holy Spirit's guidance to reveal where He first began to engraft the promises of God's new covenant into you (John 14:26). While it may feel like your mind can grasp all seven promises at once, that's rarely true. Each person connects with God through faith in a unique, personal way. From my experience and conversations with others, many connect to God through one or two of His foundational promises. These are often the promises that led you to first love Jesus Christ. As Peter explains in 2 Peter 1:3–4, they were given to you when Jesus Christ revealed His glory and excellence, drawing you to Himself. These promises became your original initial convictions of truth about Christ (Hebrews 3:14). They are the promises that the Holy Spirit spoke into your heart at the beginning of your relationship with Him. By holding onto and continuing to trust in your promises that you received from Jesus Christ, your passion for God and His will can grow, empowering you to endure in faith until the end.

On my journey, the promise that first ignited my faith and drew me closer to Him was the possibility of a personal relationship with God. As I mentioned in the Introduction, Freddy Gage's story was the catalyst that opened my eyes to the reality of God as my heavenly Father and me as His child. Being "in Christ" meant I was part of God's eternal family, a new creation with a transformed identity.

Only a few years ago, however, did I begin to *understand the blueprint path* revealed in 2 Peter 1: the new covenant promises designed for me. The impact of these truths was immediate upon my acceptance of Christ. However, I didn't realize that these promises were also His strategy to unveil my unique spiritual journey of living in His grace. These promises were given to empower me, initiating and then sustaining my participation in His divine nature—a calling for all believers. While I had embraced the gospel's truth, I had not yet recognized these promises as part of His grand and magnificent message, enabling me to partake of His divine nature and strengthen my new identity in Christ.

If you've done the math, you know I've been a Christian for over 50 years. Yet, for much of that time, I didn't realize the importance of focusing on the promises that first drew me to Christ. I accepted and believed the whole Bible, studying it diligently and seeking to understand its doctrines and applications. Still, like many Christians I shepherded, I often found myself on a spiritual roller coaster, experiencing highs of growth and lows of doubt or sin. As the apostle Paul writes in Romans 7:18, "The willingness to do good is present in me, but not the doing of the good" (ability to carry it out). I had a sincere desire to follow Christ closely but lacked the understanding of how to access the divine nature and power of the Holy Spirit through His personal path for me.

Like many believers, my spiritual experience mirrored that of the Israelites in the book of Judges. For years, I lived my Christian life in a roller-coaster fashion. I went from being passionate about God to experiencing spiritual low points. I stumbled in my faith repeatedly, only to find Him faithful each time, as I sought His help through one problem after another.

My life has been profoundly transformed by adopting the meditative trust in God's promises that He engrafted into my soul when I first believed. I began to follow God's instructions to Joshua—"This book of the Law must never depart from your mouth. Meditate on it day and night so that you may be careful to observe all that is written in it, for then you will prosper in your ways. Then you will succeed. Have I not commanded you? Be strong and courageous! Do not be afraid or discouraged, for the LORD your God is with you wherever you go" (Joshua 1:8–9). As I fixed my eyes on Jesus through my original convictions, my passion for Christ and His will in my life became a powerful force.

The Bible is often described as "meditative literature," inviting us to absorb its truths through reflection and contemplation. Embracing this discipline of meditating on God's promises has become the instruction that yokes me to Christ's life, serving as a powerful, transformative force. As I *consistently* began to meditate on the scriptural promises He has given me, my life began to change dramatically.

Looking back, I can now see how God has been shaping and nurturing my faith over time. My most significant spiritual growth and productivity emerged when the Holy Spirit enabled me to trust in the foundational promise of God as my Father. This trust was reinforced through parallel promises that revealed His character, my identity in Him, and His love for me. As I meditated on these precious promises, He was able to disciple me through my struggles. The more I intentionally and consistently sought His presence through His promises, the more my confidence in Him grew, and the more He could manifest His life through me.

Now, I realize that God was fortifying my faith, layer by layer, much like a carefully constructed building. John 15:12, "This is my commandment: Love one another as I have loved you," comes alive, instilling in me the confidence to share His truth. By focusing on how He has loved me, I am learning to follow His blueprint to become more loving towards others.

Christ's Spirit Disciples Others *through* Us

The seven principles of promise form the blueprint, which you can access every day, laying the foundation of the new covenant through faith, love, and obedience, which guide our spiritual growth. As you follow the Spirit's plan in your own life, you can also encourage others to become intentional in allowing themselves to be discipled by the Holy Spirit. As He disciples you, He will be making disciples through you. To do this, you must remember God's perspectives and promises as revealed in the blueprint of the new covenant. It's also important to remember that Jesus's teachings and discipleship were somewhat limited by Christ coming in the form of a man, as the Holy Spirit was not yet sent; therefore, the Holy Spirit could not be in them nor they in Christ until after the resurrection and ascension when the Holy Spirit came on Pentecost as recorded in Acts chapter two. The absence of the Holy Spirit dwelling in them means that we cannot base the making of disciples solely on how Jesus Christ made disciples in the gospel accounts. The historical accounts of Jesus's life, serving as a transition period between the covenants, provide us with insight into the discipling process; but not a complete picture of the process. It is crucial to understand that the discipling process under the previous covenants does not give us a comprehensive understanding of how we are being discipled now that we who believe are "in Christ" and the Holy Spirit dwells in us. The role of the Holy Spirit in the discipling process is a key aspect of the New Covenant. To fully understand this, it's necessary to include the revelation given in 2 Peter 1 and remember God's perspectives and

2 The Blueprint

promises as revealed in the blueprint of the new covenant. Understanding this will enable you to guide others by helping them recall how Jesus Christ manifested God to them through His glory and goodness and how the Spirit of Christ in them is now revealing God through the New Covenant promises.

Instead of *telling* fellow believers how to act or what promises to believe, it's more effective to ask questions about their spiritual beginnings. Listen to their story of encountering God's glory and goodness. Ask what new insights they've gained since trusting in Christ. Other questions that can help reveal a person's foundational faith include:

- Which promises in the new covenant prophecies resonate most with you?
- What are the "default" truths or verses you turn to in your lowest moments?
- How have you cultivated or continue to cultivate your relationship with God through these promises?

You can optimize your relationship with God and others by embracing the blueprint of promises found in the new covenant. The discovery questions at the end of this book will help you reflect on the ideas presented in this section. Every believer who trusts in Jesus Christ receives these blueprint promises, but the ways God personalizes them to you is explored further in chapter 3. There, we'll examine the pattern of Paul's conversion and Peter's path to an optimal life, discovering the Holy Spirit's model for living a spiritually fulfilling life.

CHAPTER 3

Peter's Path to an Optimal Life

The LORD says this: 'Stand by the crossroads and look. Ask about the ancient paths, saying, "Where is the good road?" Then walk in it, and you will find rest for your souls.
JEREMIAH 6:16

The apostle Peter's second letter is his farewell, final reminders, and warnings to the first-century church. In the first 11 verses, he describes a personal, optimal plan for every believer to excel in faith, be productive and fruitful, and overcome the evils of this world. Peter gives you a clear perspective to help you understand how the Holy Spirit has led you from the moment you first believed in Jesus Christ. The path we choose and God's path for us are not always in harmony. Yet, God's Word calls us to learn to think His thoughts, live His ways, and walk in His path.

Consider this chapter written by Peter over two thousand years ago as the Rosetta Stone of spiritual formation. Just as the Rosetta Stone unlocked the meaning of ancient Egyptian hieroglyphs when discovered by French soldiers in 1799, Peter's clear step-by-step explanation of partaking in the divine nature unlocks the path to spiritual transformation. Without it, you might try to conform Christ's image through self-effort and moralist imperatives. Keep this context in mind as you read: Peter reminds us that this transformative path was not new to first-century believers, saying, "I will always be diligent to enable you to remember these things after my departure" (2 Peter 1:15).

This perspective on spiritual formation is not a new revelation; it is God's way, in which the earliest believers were already established in knowing and following Jesus. This description of spiritual formation was likely part of the "apostles' teaching" mentioned in Acts 2:42—practices that shaped the early church in the first weeks and months following Pentecost: "They devoted themselves to the apostles' teaching and to fellowship, to meals together and to prayer." This fellowship focused on God's personal interaction with his people, creating a profound cultural impact. It can do the same today in your own journey!

Peter emphasizes that this path is the standard for spiritual formation when he writes, "I think it right, as long as I am in this body, to stir you up by way of reminder, since I know that the putting off of my body will be soon, as our Lord Jesus Christ made clear to me" (2 Peter 1:13–14 ESV). He is clearly stating that he is nearing death—these are among his final words. Peter's purpose in writing this letter is to encourage believers to stay steadfast, holding to the way they already know so that after his departure they would be able to recall his teachings and those of the other apostles.

Yet, the present-day church has often overlooked Peter's path as an internal discipleship process led by the Holy Spirit, and it is rarely central in books on spiritual formation. However, Peter's instructions reflect the way God has always discipled his leaders and people throughout Scripture. The better you grasp Peter's instructions, the more you will recognize Christ's way of discipling you—and it will improve the way you disciple others, revealing the transformative power of the Holy Spirit in your life.

To illustrate that Peter's path is the normative way of the Holy Spirit working in each believer, consider the apostle Paul's conversion recorded in Acts 9. At this point, Paul—still known as Saul—despised Christ's followers, known as the people of "the Way" (Acts 9:2). Armed with letters from the high priest, he was traveling to Damascus to find Jewish followers of "the Way" in the synagogues and bring them back to Jerusalem as prisoners. But as he neared Damascus, suddenly, a light from heaven—a clear sign of Christ's presence—flashed around him (Acts 9:3). The story continues:

> *He fell to the ground and heard a voice say to him, "Saul, Saul, why are you persecuting me?" "Who are you, Lord?" Saul asked. He replied, "I am Jesus, whom you are persecuting,*

[It is hard for you to kick against the goads.] Now get up and go to the city, and you will be told what you must do" (Acts 9:4–6).

Saul is blinded by the light and overwhelmed as he realizes he has been fighting against God. In shock and humbled into helplessness, he spends three days in blinded darkness at the house of Judas, reflecting on his life in light of this encounter. Then, the Lord Jesus Christ sends a disciple named Ananias with a personal message for Saul: "[He] is my chosen instrument to carry my name before the Gentiles and their kings and to the Israelites. I will show him how much he must suffer for my name" (Acts 9:15) Ananias obeys, prays for Saul, and his sight is restored. Saul then gets up and is baptized.

Observe what happens in Saul's life after his encounter with the risen Christ and his baptism, as you reflect on Peter's path. Before meeting Christ, Saul was known for persecuting Christians. But when Jesus revealed Himself, it was through a blinding "light from heaven"; the glory of Christ. Jesus' presence, always filled with glory, blinds us to the things of this world and opens our eyes to see the reality of the God's kingdom. Also essential to understanding Peter's path is the message of promise given to Saul. This promise became the foundation of Saul's new identity in Christ, anchoring his love for Jesus and his ***original convictions***. It was the message he would look back on as his first love and the core of his faith—what he heard from the beginning.

Paul's conversion offers a clear model for understanding the transformative path Peter describes. Peter reminds believers that he is not introducing new concepts but reinforcing what they already know about spiritual formation. Now, let's dive into Peter's words as guided by the Holy Spirit.

Finding Focus: How the Holy Spirit Leads Us *Through* Each Step

In the quotation that follows from 2 Peter 1:1–4, I've highlighted the word *through* because it serves as an entryway, showing how the Holy Spirit guides believers into a relationship with Christ and into following Him. Notice also that verses 3 and 4 form one complete, connected sentence, with each phrase linked to give a fuller picture of what Peter is communicating:

> *From Simon Peter, a servant and apostle of Jesus Christ. To those who have received a faith of the same kind as ours **through** the righteousness of our God and Savior Jesus Christ: May grace and peace be multiplied to you **through** knowing God and Jesus our Lord. His divine power has given us everything we need pertaining to life and godliness, **through** knowing him who called us by his glory and excellence, **through** which he has given us his magnificent and precious promises so that **through** them you may become partakers of the divine nature; for you have escaped the corruption that is in the world as a result of lust* (2 Peter 1:1–4, emphasis mine).

In verses 2–4, Peter emphasizes that God has given us an abundance of grace and peace and declares that "His divine power has given us everything we need pertaining to life and godliness." Grace, the action of "God who works in you to will and to work for his good pleasure" (Philippians 2:13), is the cornerstone of our spiritual growth and a reminder that we are never alone in our journey. Peace, the spiritual harmony we experience with God and others as we humble ourselves before Him, strengthens our hope. Together, grace and peace, along with everything needed for life and godliness, form a complete portion of spiritual power.

Yet, despite this abundant provision, many believers struggle to make progress in their spiritual lives. When they rely on self-effort or self-help methods, they can feel as hopeless as orphans. Others may struggle because they doubt the truth of the Bible. Why is there a gap between the abundant life God has given us and the spiritually weak lives many Christians lead? The answer is that they have "abandoned" their first love for Jesus and His personal guidance, missing the opportunity to partake of the divine nature consistently. Without Jesus, we can do nothing; we need His divine power to "[work] in you (us) to will and to work for his good pleasure," which is God's grace in action (Philippians 2:13).

God is not powerless. As Peter affirms, He has given us everything we need for a godly life, along with the same kind of faith as the apostles (2 Peter 1:1, 3)! To experience the abundant life God desires for you, it's essential to learn how to access the spiritual power of Christ. You first accessed this grace as you encountered his glory and humbled yourself before Him to partake of the divine nature. This connection continues as you abide in "what you have heard from the beginning" (1 John 2:24).

The evidence of partaking of "the divine nature" is a *continued and growing* love for God, an increase in spiritual fruit, and a life lived for His glory. Understanding how to abide in Christ is not merely a suggestion; it is essential for spiritual growth. It's the key to feeling secure and connected in your optimal faith journey.

Jesus Gives Us a Personal Doorway to the Father.

Second Peter 1:1–4 teaches that you came to know Jesus Christ personally when He called you by His glory and excellence into His kingdom. In these first four verses, the word ***through*** appears five times, each instance highlighting the way God reveals Himself to you and deepens your knowledge of Him. Each ***through*** is like an open door, inviting you to step repeatedly into participation with the divine nature and into life in Christ. ***Through*** His glory and goodness, you receive precious promises that become your spiritual sustenance, enabling you to partake of His divine nature. Just as a mother's milk nourishes a newborn, God invites you to interact with His holy nature for spiritual nourishment and growth in Christ. This partaking of God is not a one-time event but an ongoing process of continually receiving His life and strength.

Peter then shows us the clear implication of this truth and the path the Holy Spirit lays out. He says, "For this very reason" (2 Peter 1:5), pointing you to where you should focus to partake of God's divine nature. This divine nature, with its transformative power, is the key to working out what God has planted within you. It should fill you with a sense of empowerment and hope, knowing that God is actively working in you. As the apostle Paul writes, "*Work out your salvation* with fear and trembling, for it is God who works in you to will and to work for his good pleasure" (Philippians 2:12–13, emphasis mine).

God calls you to build upon your faith (2 Peter 1:5). The spiritual fruit He seeks serves as evidence that you are truly His disciple. Peter explains that this fruit is produced as you *partake of the divine nature*, cultivating the seeds of promise God has planted in you. Through the Spirit's empowerment, you are then able to "make every effort to add to your faith":

- Moral Excellence (righteous behavior)
- Knowledge (growing in knowing Jesus personally)
- Self-control (humility disciplines that glorify God)
- Endurance (perseverance in faithfulness)
- Godliness (manifesting Christ-like character)
- Mutual Affection (empathy and compassion toward others)
- Love (unconditional goodwill to all people)
(2 Peter 1:5–7)

"For if these qualities are in you and increasing, they will keep you from being ineffective and unproductive in the knowledge of our Lord Jesus Christ" (2 Peter 1:8). A genuine spiritual life reveals itself in a fruitful life, characterized by these qualities, which mark an optimal life. As verse 9 warns, "Whoever does not have these qualities is blind—nearsighted, having forgotten that they received purification from their past sins."

If you continually focus on your sins and failings rather than on Christ and His promises, you will struggle to build upon your faith. Jesus said in John 15:5, "For apart from me you cannot produce anything." Without His divine nature sustaining your faith, it cannot produce the fruit of the Spirit. Only a Christ-centered focus, grounded in His promises, can develop Christ's character in you. When you lack the qualities Peter describes, it often stems from a self-focused approach, believing you must produce righteousness on your own rather than trusting in the eternal life God offers through partaking in Christ's divine nature.

Peter urges, "So, brothers and sisters, be diligent to make your calling and election firm, for by doing this you will never stumble; and this way you will receive a rich welcome into the eternal kingdom of our Lord and Savior Jesus Christ" (2 Peter 1:10–11).

The "diligence" Peter refers to means intentionally focusing on Christ by meditating on and abiding in the promises that brought you into Him and all He provides. This path of partaking in the divine nature is the same path Paul followed and taught the first-century believers. He writes in Colossians 3:1–4, "If then you have been raised with Christ seek the things above, where Christ is seated at the right hand of God; set your minds on things above and not on the things on earth, for you have died and your life is hidden with Christ in God the Father. When Christ, who is your life, appears, then you also will appear with him in glory." Diligently set your heart and mind on the promises He has given you; they are your guiding light in your spiritual journey.

How You Perceive Glory Is Essential

Do you know what God's glory is? It's Him revealing Himself to you. Every encounter with Jesus Christ, the living God, is an encounter with his goodness, love, forgiveness, peace, and more. Every quality that describes God is a facet of His glory. The qualities Peter encourages you to "make every effort to add to your faith" (2 Peter 1:5) are simply the fruit of experiencing His glory within your soul. Paul describes this transformative process in 2 Corinthians 3:17–18:

> *Now the Lord is the Spirit, and where the Spirit of the Lord is, there is freedom from the laws demands. And we all, with unveiled faces, see the Lord's glory as in a mirror and are being transformed into the same image (i.e., his image) with ever-increasing glory. This is from the Lord, who is the Spirit.*

From glory to glory, He is transforming you.

Reflect on how you have experienced the Lord's glory. Can you recognize moments when His goodness or virtue led you to repentance and surrender? Think back to when you first experienced God's grace and peace. What was happening in your life when God's glory and goodness first broke through and touched you? This may have been the first time you fully surrendered, your heart warmed to Jesus Christ, and you received Him. If so, it marked your first love experience with God's Son—a moment when Jesus became personal and real, imparting promises of grace that revealed His love to you and gave you hope to trust Christ for eternity.

John describes this as receiving a different kind of life, called "eternal life" (1 John 2:25).

How vividly do you remember your first love for Jesus? What new covenant truths or promises resonated with your heart? These might include promises of forgiveness, redemption, or eternal life. These original promises form the foundation of your convictions (see Hebrews 3:12–14; 8:8–12). Continuing to abide in these original foundational truths is essential for sustaining your spiritual growth.

To intentionally cultivate the spiritual fruit or qualities Peter describes, you must hold firmly to the truth you first believed. John writes, "As for you, let what you have heard from the beginning remain in you. If it does, you also will remain in the Son and in the Father. And this is the promise he promised us—eternal life" (1 John 2:24–25).

Paul offered a similar exhortation to the early church in Colossians 1:21–23, emphasizing the importance of holding steadfastly to their faith:

> *And although you were formerly alienated and hostile in your thoughts, engaged in evil deeds, Christ has now reconciled you to God the Father through his body of flesh, through death, in order to present you before him holy and blameless and beyond reproach, if indeed you* **continue in the faith, established and steadfast, and do not move away from the hope of the gospel that you heard,** *which has been proclaimed in all creation under heaven, and of which I, Paul, have become a minister"* (emphasis mine).

This first epiphany—your spiritual revelation of who God is and who you are in Christ—is vital for your spiritual development. Notice how often Scripture emphasizes the importance of holding on to your original promises, what you heard from the beginning, and your foundational convictions.

The writer of Hebrews highlights these original convictions as critical for keeping us from hardening our hearts and drifting away from God:

> *Take care, brothers and sisters, that there never be in any of you an evil, unbelieving heart that leads you to fall away*

from the living God. Rather, encourage one another daily, as long as it is called "today" so that none of you will be hardened by the deceitfulness of sin. For we have become participants in the life of Christ, if indeed we hold firmly to our original conviction till the end" (Hebrews 3:12–14).

When you first believed and became a partaker or participant in the life of Christ, it was through the promises that resonated within you. The lasting result of this initial encounter—your first love for Jesus Christ—was joy. Joy is the bliss of knowing you are accepted by God, the delight of knowing that you are forgiven, loved, and chosen for a life of purpose. It is the realization that you are now in God's favor, enjoying His presence, with a new identity in Christ, and His Spirit now within you. This joy is the evidence of your first love for Jesus Christ.

Joy is the flower of assured hope. "Hope deferred sickens the heart, but a longing fulfilled is a tree of life" (Proverbs 13:12). When you believe and receive Jesus, you experience the fulfillment of your heart's deepest longings, as though partaking from the tree of life—a blessing and source of God's eternal life and goodness. Receiving Christ is always a joyful blessing! True biblical hope and joy come from the awareness that God's will is being fulfilled in and through you. When Christians lack joy, it often means they have shifted their spiritual focus from Jesus and lost the delight that comes from living in God's presence.

It is no surprise, then, that the glorified Christ rebukes the Ephesian church for their critical failure in abandoning their love and joy in Him: "I have this against you: You have departed from your initial love of me. Think about how far you've fallen! Repent. Do the works you did at first. If you do not, I am coming to you and will remove your lampstand from its place—if you do not repent" (Revelation 2:4–5). Christ calls us to remember His promises of hope, to embrace who He is and who we are in Him, and to return to loving Him fully. Each magnificent and precious promise is your doorway to discovering your unique path in following God. Every encounter with God's glory and goodness invites you to seek and hold onto the great promises He has given you.

Your relationship with God—the personal and unique connection you have through being in Christ—began when he called you by His glory and goodness. You experienced the personal attention of the God of the universe, who gave you great and precious promises of hope. The word *precious* signifies the value and worth of these promises. Just as gold is precious, so are God's promises to you. These words from God are filled with life and are meant to be your personal guide—promises on which you are to meditate and abide, so they may become a "lamp to guide [your] feet, a light on [your] path" (Psalm 119:105). The promises He has given you form your unique and optimal pathway to knowing Him and living out your identity in Christ.

Have you recognized the promises He has given you? He calls them "magnificent and precious" (2 Peter 1:4). Are they precious to you? What have you done with them?

God intends for these precious promises to be a guiding light on your path. Have they become that for you? Too often, Christians receive God's magnificent promises with joy at first, but later neglect or forget them when striving to follow Jesus more closely. Losing delight in His promises leads to a loss of joy and passion for His will.

Peter teaches that through these precious promises, we can connect to and participate in God's divine nature if we choose to! Ponder that: it's a profound gift. You and I are invited into loving fellowship with God Almighty, with our risen Savior, Jesus Christ our Lord. Yet, sadly, many believers seldom abide in the promises given to them to live an abundant, joy-filled life with Him.

When you hold fast to your unique, precious promises, you continually break free from the darkness of this world and walk in the light of His glory. This is living optimally in Christ, the path of transformation into His image, proving the good and perfect will of God.

Peter then describes the effects of partaking of Christ's divine nature through these promises. You will "add" to your faith, much like a healthy tree naturally bears fruit on each branch. Peter's list can be compared to the fruit of the Spirit that Paul gives us in Galatians 5:22, "The fruit of the Spirit is love, joy, peace, patience, kindness, goodness, faithfulness, gentleness, and self-control." It's clear that Peter and Paul are expressing the same spiritual truth: partaking in the divine nature leads to the same spiritual growth as walking in the Spirit.

When you connect and abide in Christ through God's promises, you will begin to grow the spiritual fruit He desires. You'll experience the abundant life filled with grace and peace that He has promised. It is no surprise that Paul says in Galatians 5:22, "Against such things there is no law." No spiritual law can resist or hinder God's power within you when you partake of his divine nature! The more you engage with the divine nature, the more resurrection life will flow through you, revealing Christ's character increasingly in your life.

This approach to spiritual formation is far from passive; it invites active engagement in your relationship with Christ. That's why Peter so strongly urges us to "make every effort to add to [our] faith (2 Peter 1:5). When we focus on Jesus through His promises, we'll find joy and strength, allowing Him to work within us to desire and fulfill God's will.

Peter then states two more spiritual principles—one incredibly positive, the other strikingly negative:

- "For if these [fruit of the Spirit] are in you and increasing, they will keep you from being ineffective and unproductive in the knowledge of our Lord Jesus Christ" (2 Peter 1:8).

- "For whoever does not have these qualities is blind—nearsighted, having forgotten that they received purification from their past sins" (2 Peter 1:9).

Peter concludes that as we focus on Jesus and follow His path for spiritual growth, we will confirm our calling of being chosen by God. As we seek the Lord wholeheartedly and intentionally, personally engaging with the promises and personal messages He has given us, we will strengthen our faith and, in so doing, gain an additional promise that we will not stumble in our trust of Jesus Christ. Furthermore, Peter says we will be welcomed with open arms into the eternal kingdom of our Lord and Savior Jesus Christ" (2 Peter 1:10–11).

Peter's path provides a vision of the optimal life available to faithful followers of Christ. It is God's invitation to live each day glorifying Him, with the promise of a rich welcome into the eternal kingdom. Peter's teaching serves as the Rosetta Stone of spiritual formation, empowering us to understand how God has discipled us and will continue to do so. As you walk in Peter's path, his guidance will become a reality in your life. You'll learn to discern your precious promises and actively engage in God's ways, participating in the divine nature.

This participation is accomplished through spiritual disciplines such as prayer, Bible study, meditation, and abiding in the promises you have in Christ. By partaking in the divine nature through these promises, you release the power of the Holy Spirit to live and love through you. The better you understand how the Holy Spirit has led you, the more empowered you become to cooperate with His present work in your life, and the better equipped you are to help others discover how Christ has been discipling them through the guidance of the Holy Spirit.

CHAPTER 4

Discerning Your Promise(s): The Gifts from His Glory and Goodness

Therefore, beloved, since we have these promises, let's cleanse ourselves from everything that can defile body and spirit, perfecting holiness in the fear of God.
2 CORINTHIANS 7:1

Optimal disciples are not satisfied with simply knowing God's promises; they desire to live them to honor Him. The first step in optimizing our relationship with God is recognizing how He *has been* discipling you to become all He designed you to be. In 2 Peter 1:1–11 we find the optimal pathway to a fruitful and productive life. Peter declares what believers have received in Christ Jesus: a faith of equal standing with the apostles, given through the righteousness of our God and Savior, Jesus Christ. This gift of faith, through His promises, enables you to access all God has for you.

Pause and consider what you've been given. All who believe in Jesus Christ have "a faith of the same kind as ours" (2 Peter 1:1), with "ours" referring to Peter and other Christian leaders of his time. It's not presumptuous to believe you can be as fruitful or effective in building the kingdom as the apostles. After all, Jesus Himself said, "I'm telling you the truth: Anyone who believes in me will do the works I have done, and they'll do greater works than these, because I'm going to the Father" (John 14:12). It's no surprise, then, that we share the same kind of faith as the apostles.

As a believer, you also receive grace and peace in increasing measure through your personal and experiential knowledge of Jesus Christ. Peter affirms, "His divine power has given us everything we need pertaining to life and godliness" (2 Peter 1:3).

You have all you need to live an abundant, fruitful, and joyful life. Peter expresses these truths in the past tense: this faith and abundant life *were already* given to you the moment you trusted in Christ's finished work. Yet, many sincere Christians don't experience this abundant life because they haven't followed Peter's pathway. If you desire an optimal relationship with God, walk in His ways as revealed by Peter's path.

Peter's path describes a deeply personal process through which Christ is discipling you. Your faith in Christ has not only saved you *but also* placed you in Him—within a new spiritual family with a heavenly Father. You now live in a new place, the kingdom of his dear Son. Once, you lived in the domain of darkness, but now you are spiritually in a different realm than you were as an unbeliever.

Your spiritual relationship of being "in Christ" is as unique as your natural dwelling place. I grew up in South Florida, and within the first year after my conversion, I moved to South Texas, where I lived for 50 years. Now, I live in Northeast Tennessee. Occasionally, I meet someone from Texas, and the question always arises: where did you live in Texas? Texas is a big place with coastal areas, deserts, hill country, plains, forests, and even mountains. Knowing where in Texas a person lives helps to understand their experiences there. I lived in San Antonio, experiencing the nearby hill country but not the mountains. San Antonio's clay, for instance, can cause significant damage to building foundations, while areas south of the city have sugar-fine, sandy soil. My experience of Texas differed depending on where I made my home.

Similarly, the kingdom of God is vast and diverse. Being "in Christ" places you in this kingdom, yet my question for believers is: where do you dwell within the kingdom? It all depends on where you choose to focus your heart and mind. Where does your heart call "home"? To find out, ask yourself these questions:

- Where do you make your mind's home in the kingdom of God?
- Does your thinking live in the confidence of Christ's forgiveness?

- Does your heart make its home in the assurance of His love?
- Does your spirit enjoy the joy of His presence?

Or perhaps, even while in Christ, your heart may dwell in a different place, if you:

- Focus too often on the fear of His disapproval,
- Dwell on your lack of faith and passion for God's kingdom, or
- Allow yourself to be consumed by negative thoughts of all kinds.

There are countless ways to experience life, even as someone in Christ. Focusing on the promises that reveal God's goodness is essential if you want to enjoy His Kingdom. These promises help you connect deeply with his presence and understand your identity in Christ, filling you with hope and encouragement.

Paul's instructions in Colossians 3:1–4 resonate with Peter's path in setting our minds on the precious promises God has given us. The more we intentionally choose to remember the reality of the new covenant in which we live, the greater the joy of our salvation will be. This leads to an important question: If I want to "seek the things above," experiencing life in Christ and enjoying God's kingdom, what should I "set" my mind on?

Just as recalling my experiences in Texas can transport me back in memory, reflecting on Christ's promises can transform you as you remember His glory and goodness. How do you truly experience life in Christ and partake of His nature? Peter explains that this happens through the promises Jesus gave when you encountered His glory. He states that the way to partake of God's divine life is through your faith in his "magnificent and precious promises" (2 Peter 1:4), which He gave you when He called you by His glory and excellence.

This is the key that fits in the lock.

What you'll read next explains ***how*** you can optimize your Christian life. When you allow the Holy Spirit to guide you, He will help you *discern and recognize* the times you have experienced—and should continue to experience—His glory and goodness. As you remember and embrace how

Jesus revealed Himself to you through His goodness and the precious message He gave you, you can more intentionally cooperate with the Holy Spirit's personal development plan for your life. This awareness will help you focus on God's promises, allowing you to intentionally cultivate these truths in your mind, heart, and spirit. Identifying moments of His glory and goodness is crucial, as these are when you received (and will continue to receive and personalize) His great and precious promises, enabling you to partake of Christ's divine nature. Remember, His promises are not just valuable like gold, silver, or precious stones—they are transformative with the power to change your life.

Discerning Your God-Given Promises Starts with His Glory

To discern your God-given promises, you must be able to articulate and understand what the word "glory" truly means. It can signify radiance, magnificence, splendor, or fame. While these words describe "glory," they don't fully capture how you experience God's glory. Think of God's glory as His light—a light by which you see the world and yourself clearly. You need this divine light to perceive and truly know Him. Every time you encounter Jesus Christ and experience His goodness, deepening your understanding of God, you're experiencing the light of His glory and the revealing of Himself and God's kingdom.

Imagine being lost in a place of utter darkness, like a deep cave. In such darkness, you can't even see your hand in front of your face. This pitch-black environment mirrors the state of our souls before knowing Christ. How would you hope to escape? Your eyes would search for even the faintest glimmer of light, for that light would become precious in your desire to be set free. But a mere pinpoint of light wouldn't be enough to guide your whole body to freedom. This is why we need the fullness of God's light, found in Jesus. In that dark cave, even the spark of light would inspire you to seek its source, hoping to find the way out. Our Father in heaven has revealed this path to freedom through Jesus. God's glory is the light that pierces the darkness and shows you the way to freedom through His goodness.

Paul describes our journey to faith in Christ using this same metaphor. In Colossians 1:12–13, he writes, "Giving thanks to the Father, who has qualified you to share in the inheritance of the saints living in light, who has rescued us from the domain of darkness, and who has transferred us into the kingdom of his beloved Son." Paul uses this image of light again in 2 Corinthians 4:6, "For God, who said, 'Let light shine out of darkness,' made his light shine in our hearts to give us the light of the knowledge of God's glory that is seen in the face of Christ."

How did God accomplish this? Reflect on your journey to Christ. Recall the steps you took, the people, and the events that finally led you to see the light and recognize that Jesus Christ is God and loves you. These moments were like small beams of His glory and goodness, guiding you from the domain of darkness into His glorious kingdom.

In Matthew 11:25–30, we see a connection between Jesus revealing the Father to people and how the promises He gives become a guiding light in your life:

> *At that time, Jesus prayed, "I praise you, Father, Lord of Heaven and earth, because you've hidden these things from the wise and intelligent and revealed them to little children. Yes, Father, for this was pleasing in your sight. All things have been handed over to me by my Father. No one knows the Son except the Father, and no one knows the Father except the Son and those to whom the Son chooses to reveal him."*

In these verses, we learn that Jesus has been given authority to reveal the Father to those He chooses. This revelation requires spiritual light—another way of saying that Jesus' glory reveals God to you. In the following verses, Jesus explains that He will reveal the Father to all who come to Him.

> *Come to me, all you who are weary and are heavily burdened, and I will give you rest. Take my yoke upon you and learn from me, for I am gentle and humble in heart, and "you will find rest for your souls." For my yoke is easy, and my burden is light*
> (Matthew 11:28–30).

Jesus reveals the Father by calling to those who are weary, burdened, and humble—those who are poor in spirit and ready to receive. These are people who are tired of relying on their own limited wisdom and strength. Coming to Jesus requires a childlike humility, an openness to receiving His guidance. To those who come, He offers spiritual light—His glory—and invites them to take on His yoke, where He becomes their guide and teacher. Through this, He reveals the Father and gives them the spiritual rest found in His love.

Jesus' Yoke Is a Metaphor for His Promises

A yoke is a tool that binds the strength of two animals, like a pair of oxen, so they can work together more effectively. When Jesus speaks of His yoke, He invited you to be bound to Him, walking in His ways. That is what His promises accomplish when you embrace them. They connect you to Jesus, revealing who God is and who you are in Him. Just as a yoke guides oxen to be more productive, God's promises, when received and allowed to work within you, produce much fruit. As Peter explains, through God's promises, you *may partake* of His divine nature. This participation fills you with the grace and passion to follow Him. Unlike a yoked animal that has no choice, you have the freedom to deliberately choose to partake in God's divine nature. Those who do so will find their walk with Christ becoming ever more fulfilling and optimal.

As you turn to Jesus, beholding His glory and accepting His promises as your yoke, you will learn from Him. This yoke is the pathway to finding rest for your soul, to understanding more deeply who He is and who you are in Him. Seeing Jesus means seeing the Father; knowing the Father through the Son also means knowing who you are *in* the Son. These promises yoke you to Christ, guiding you to rest in your new identity of being a child of God.

Learning from Him through this yoke is another way of describing the process of partaking of the divine nature. As you abide in Him and live by His promises, God's Spirit transforms you into the image of Christ. The more you see God's glory through His promises, the more you partake of His nature. Every moment of revelation, every insight given by His Spirit and His Word, brings His life and light into your heart and mind—this is His glory. As John writes in his gospel, "In [Jesus Christ] was life, and that life was the light of all humanity" (John 1:4).

Peter, James, and John See Jesus' Glory

The Bible provides insight into glory and its transformative impact on our lives. God unveiled the glory of Jesus Christ in His transfiguration on the mountain with Peter, James, and John. This awe-inspiring event is captured in the Gospels of Matthew, Mark, and Luke, where Jesus invites the disciples to join him on the mountain to pray. As he prayed, he was transfigured, radiating the majestic splendor of God's glory:

> *Six days later, Jesus took Peter, James, and John and led them up a high mountain all by themselves. There he was transfigured in front of them. His clothes became dazzling white, whiter than any launderer on earth can whiten. And Elijah and Moses appeared to them and were talking with Jesus. Peter said to Jesus, "Rabbi, it is good for us to be here. Let's put up three temporary shelters: one for you, one for Moses, and one for Elijah." Peter didn't know what to say, for they were terrified. Then a cloud formed and came over them, and a voice came out of it: "This is my beloved Son. Listen to him!" And suddenly, when they looked around, they no longer saw anyone with them except Jesus* (Mark 9:2–8).

In each Gospel account, Jesus' divine, glorious nature is revealed, leaving the three disciples in awe. They see him not only as their Teacher but as the Holy Son of God, radiant in heavenly light. Peter's reaction shows a natural human response to the overwhelming presence of God. Attempting to contain this extraordinary experience within his religious understanding, he suggests building shelters for Jesus, Moses, and Elijah. This reveals how we often try to fit revelations of God's glory into our own frameworks, when we are unable to fully grasp the magnificence of what we've encountered. God's glory shatters our finite understanding, reminding us that some truths are beyond our comprehension. The voice from heaven directs the disciples—and us—to simply listen and follow Jesus.

Like Peter, when you encounter God's glory, it can indeed be overwhelming, even frightening. The Old Testament prophet Isaiah was undone by God's holiness in Isaiah 6; Paul was struck down on the road to Damascus in Acts 9; and John fell as though dead when he saw the risen Christ in Revelation. Such moments humble us profoundly, reminding us that we are in the presence of the living King. Often, the experience leaves a lasting mark, transforming us with a deeper understanding of God's goodness—whether through hope, love, joy, peace, forgiveness, or mercy. Every encounter with his glory and goodness is a call to repentance and a *powerful catalyst for your ongoing transformation, filling you with* hope and encouragement.

These experiences instill a renewed, humble faith and a deeper understanding of who God is, who you are, and how He loves you personally. Encounters with God's glory impart precious promises and lasting truths that encourage and guide us. When we engraft these revelations into our hearts, they *continually* define God's reality and reveal a pathway to further partake of His divine nature.

Peter Experiences God's Glory

In 2 Peter 1, the apostle Peter not only explains how you can enter this path of fruitfulness but also reveals how seeing Jesus' glory at the transfiguration impacted his whole life. Years later, he writes about his experience:

> *For we were eyewitnesses of his majesty. We did not follow cleverly devised tales when we made known to you the power and the coming of our Lord Jesus Christ. We ourselves heard a voice brought from heaven when we were with him on the sacred mountain. He received honor and glory from God the Father when that voice came to him from the Majestic Glory, saying, "This is my Son, whom I love, with whom I am well pleased"* (2 Peter 1:16–18).

Peter, James, and John all saw the transfiguration of the man Jesus into the glorious Son of God, an experience that terrified them. At that moment, the Father spoke a powerful, promise-filled truth that Peter would desperately need later to become an optimal follower of Jesus: "This is my Son, whom I love, with whom I am well pleased."

This truth became a stabilizing promise to guide Peter through the confusing and dreadful disappointment of denying Christ three times (Luke 22:54–62). The Holy Spirit actively utilized the revelation of the transfigured Son of God and the powerful words spoken by God the Father to disciple and transform Peter. This is a divine plan that each of us can—and should—experience. This promise enabled him to stand firm in his faith and repent to the point of tears on the night he denied Jesus. Later, after Jesus' resurrection and Pentecost, Peter connected the revelation of Jesus' glory at the transfiguration and the Old Testament prophecies of the coming Messiah into a powerful sermon—through which 3,000 "souls were added to the church that day" (Acts 2:41).

Focus on the Big Picture

Often, as sincere believers, we don't understand the larger context of why God answers our prayers. We can miss the promises the Holy Spirit is giving us to yoke us to Jesus for His glory. Many times, we only want to escape a problem or relieve our pain, weariness, and burdens. Then, after the issue is resolved, we return to the same lifestyle that caused the unrest. By not understanding how God is working in our lives, we can drift away from our love of Jesus—with dire consequences. If you don't allow God to keep you yoked to Jesus through the promises He's given you, you'll find it challenging to add to your faith, as Peter taught the first-century believers. The book of Judges illustrates this behavior of not trusting God. The Israelites repeated the cycles of sinning, entering bondage, turning to God, and receiving deliverance. The book of Joshua illustrates the opposite behavior. Joshua meditated and stayed yoked to the promises the Lord gave him, and he led the Jews into the victory God had promised.

To be an optimal disciple, it's important to remember how God has been discipling you through the encounters you have with His glory, considering every precious promise from Him as a personal seed word or yoke from Christ. Your yoke from Jesus will give you spiritual rest—but do not stop there. You then need to take the yoke of his promise and

4 Discerning Your Promise

allow Him to teach you His ways, continually making the prayer in Psalm 86:11–12 your own:

> *O LORD, teach me your ways that I may walk in your truth;*
> *unite my divided heart to fear your name. O Lord my God,*
> *I will praise you with all my heart, and I will glorify your*
> *name forevermore.*

At the end of his life, Peter reflects on his supernatural experience at the transfiguration, connecting it to the Father's declaration, "This is my Son, whom I love, with whom I am well pleased" (2 Peter 1:17). Peter aligns this experience with the prophetic word of Scripture. Together, the internal revelation and the external prophecies about the Messiah confirm the transformative truth that Jesus Christ is God come in the flesh. This harmony of subjective experience and objective truth is powerful. As Peter says, "We also have the prophetic word made certain, and you will do well to pay attention, as to a light shining in a dark place, until the day dawns and Christ, the morning star, rises in your hearts" (2 Peter 1:19). These promises were Peter's guiding lights, sustaining him through the dark moments of his life as he pursued his purpose and destiny.

We may never see Jesus transfigured as Peter did, but all who come to Christ and receive the yoke of His promises may learn from Him and be transformed. Reflect on these questions:

- Do you remember when God's presence first became real to you—when you felt the transformative power of His glory? (Think of when you first felt the hope and assurance of His love and grace.)
- How did His presence, glory, and goodness change your life?
- In that moment, what verse, message of truth, or promise did God impress on your heart?
- What are you doing with it today? Are you reflecting on this promise of hope, faith, or love regularly?

That first epiphany from God was your personal contact with Christ's glory, meant to become a "lamp to guide [your] feet, a light on [your] path" (Psalm 119:105). Remember, when He reveals His glory to you, it marks not only *the beginning* of your transformation but also your ongoing transformation into His Son's image. Have you planted that seed/truth message in your heart and cultivated it with tears of joy, the sunshine of praise, and the water of thanksgiving? If so, then the fruit of that seed now nourishes you, providing spiritual bread and seeds for you to sow into the hearts of others (Isaiah 55:10–11).

All true believers have moments when they experience God's glory. As you humbly seek the Lord Jesus through His Word and Spirit, you should also have new encounters. As you seek him, His glory can break into your life at any moment, offering you great and magnificent promises. Yet, you will experience his presence *more deeply and bear more fruit* if you commit to a disciplined pursuit of Him.

Each time you experience God's glory and goodness, become aware of His presence and seek His promises. Psalm 139:17–18 tells us that God continually pours out gracious thoughts towards us*:* "How precious also are your thoughts about me, O God; how great is the sum of them! If I counted them, they would be more than the sand. And when I wake up, you are still with me." Just as the sun beams down daily, God's glory shines on you. The more you embrace His goodness through His personalized promises to you, the more your joy, passion, and hope will grow!

The psalmist's prayer in Psalm 119:49–50, "Remember your word to your servant, in which you have made me hope. It is my comfort in my trouble; your word (promise) revives me" (addition mine), reflects the personal nature of God's promises. Each one is a testament to His love and care for you.

When you abide in the promises of God, they kindle a passion for Him and His purpose for your life. Imagine how your life would change if you intentionally cultivated the great and precious promises personally given to you by Jesus Christ! This abiding discipline is the optimal path to spiritual growth that many Christians overlook. Many believers neglect the promises God has given them, not out of willful disobedience, but often from a lack of understanding of how Christ is discipling them. By cultivating these seeds of promise, your passion for God will deepen, you will bear greater fruit, and your obedience to the Holy Spirit will increase. In turn, you'll begin to love others more fully, as He loves them.

In each of these moments, when God's glory pierces the darkness of your life, He gives you another message of His grace and goodness. Each beam of His glorious grace is a point of light, illuminating a fuller picture of your God and King. The question that determines your fruitfulness as a follower of Jesus is, "What did you do with your promises?"

Now that you are beginning to see the power of God's promises to you, consider how He has prepared the soil of your life— your heart, mind, and body—to be the perfect garden for bearing much fruit and bringing glory to our God and King, Jesus Christ.

CHAPTER 5

How God Prepared the Soil of Your Soul to Become an Optimal Disciple

But the one sown on good soil, this is one who both hears the word and understands it, thus bearing fruit—producing a hundred, sixty, or thirty times what was sown.
MATTHEW 13:23

There are many gardening metaphors used to illustrate spiritual growth and life in the Bible. Jesus frequently described the kingdom of God through these vivid agricultural illustrations. In John 15, He declares that He is the true vine and His Father is the gardener. Similarly, when Jesus curses the fruitless fig tree in Matthew 21:19, He highlights God's judgment against the spiritual barrenness He saw in Israel. One of the most striking and insightful metaphors for spiritual growth is the Word of God as seed and the believer's heart or soul as soil. The Parable of the Sower, recorded in all three Synoptic Gospels, offers a foundational account of this spiritual truth.

In this parable, found in Matthew 13, Mark 4, and Luke 8, the seeds represent the words or promises of God. The sower, who is God, scatters the seed across various types of soil, each representing a different condition of the heart. While the seed remains the same, the soils differ in their ability to nurture it and produce fruit. This highlights the critical importance of preparing and cultivating the soil of our hearts and souls to ensure spiritual fruitfulness.

5 How God Prepared the Soil of Your Soul

Cultivating a Fruitful Garden

From 2004 to 2017, Eunice and I lived south of San Antonio, Texas, in what is known as the sand country of Wilson County. The soil there was sugar-fine sand that could blow like dust across our yard on a hot, dry Texas day. I dreamed of growing a vegetable garden, so I had the soil tested for nutrients. The results were discouraging—it was completely barren with no significant nutrients. The experts told me that without adding organic material and fertilizer to the soil, my hope of a fruitful garden would be futile. Even with the best seeds, the soil, as it was, would never produce the desired harvest.

Guided by the advice of my local garden center, I learned how to prepare the soil. I built raised beds and enriched the barren soil with nutrients, fertilizers, and compost. Over time, what was once lifeless dirt became fertile ground that yielded an abundance of delicious fruits and vegetables.

Thankfully, the God who has called us to Himself is also a master gardener. In John 15:1, Jesus says, "My Father is the vineyard keeper." Just as a gardener carefully prepares the soil to ensure a fruitful harvest, God has lovingly prepared you with the same intimate care and intentionality, as described in the intricacy of our creation in Psalm 139.

You may not fully realize the astounding process of your creation. David describes how God watches over and intricately forms each person in the womb. Understanding how personally God created you is essential to appreciating why and how Christ revealed Himself to you and why you have been given specific promises from God, as described in 2 Peter 1:4. The more you grasp how God formed you in your mother's womb, the more your hope and confidence will grow, empowering you to trust the promises He has made.

You can rest assured in knowing God has deliberately chosen every detail of your life. He has providentially guided you through both blessings and trials to conform you to the image of His Son. Reflecting on the purpose and care behind your creation should fill you with confidence that the One, "who began a good work in you will bring it to completion until the day of Christ Jesus" (Philippians 1:6).

Every believer experiences God's glory and goodness in a uniquely personal way. Your distinctive experience of the revelation of Jesus Christ is deeply connected to the way God uniquely created you. Scripture teaches that He prepared your heart to receive Him even before the foundation of the world. As Ephesians 2:10 reminds us, "For we are his handiwork, created in Christ Jesus for good works, which God prepared in advance, that you should walk in them."

The magnificent and precious promises Peter describes in 2 Peter 1:3–4 are like perfect seeds designed to thrive in the soil of your soul. When God intricately and uniquely formed you in your mother's womb, He also considered the specific promises—truths about His character and nature—that you would need to cultivate Christ's character within you. Just as a skilled gardener understands the purpose of each seed and the characteristics of the soil to ensure a fruitful harvest, God, the perfect gardener, in His infinite wisdom, knows your destiny and precisely what you need to fulfill your God-given purpose.

Every human gardener understands that without seeds, no plant or fruit can grow. Similarly, you can't produce the fruit of the Spirit by your own strength or effort. This truth aligns perfectly with John 1:12–13, which explains how we are born into the kingdom—not by human effort, but by the will and work of God: "To all who did receive him, to those who believed in his name, he gave the right to become children of God, born, not of human descent, nor of sexual desire, nor of human's decision, but born of God." Paul adds to our knowledge about our spiritual beginning and growth when he writes in Colossians 2:6–7, "Walk in Christ Jesus the Lord, just as you have received him." To know that God is involved in every step of your spiritual development, from beginning to end, is a critical truth in trusting your heavenly Father.

The Parable of the Sower teaches, "The seed is the word of God" (Luke 8:11). The promises you have already received are magnificent seeds of life for your Spirit. They empower you to be fruitful, glorifying God with the fruit of the Spirit. As you intentionally "become partakers of His divine nature" (2 Peter 1:4), you fulfill the role of the productive soil in the Parable of the Sower and the fruitful branches Jesus describes in John 15. By participating in His divine nature through His promises, abiding in His Word, and cultivating His truth, His life flows through you to produce abundant fruit, revealing you are His faithful disciple (John 15:1–17).

This is why the apostle Peter speaks so confidently in 2 Peter 1:5–10, urging believers to be diligent and make every effort to understand God's path. He assures you that when you participate in God's divine nature through the promises He has given you, you can expect a productive and abundant life. God desires this for us—a life that "will keep you from being ineffective and unproductive in the knowledge of our Lord Jesus Christ." (2 Peter 1:8)

As you abide in Him and His great and precious promises, you can rely on His work in you—not only for your initial entrance into His kingdom but also for discerning His thoughts and walking daily in His way. Your confidence in spiritual growth rests on His divine nature and power, as you keep "fixing [y]our eyes on Jesus, the author, and perfecter of [y]our faith" (Hebrews 12:2).

Psalm 139:13–18 beautifully reveals the step-by-step process of how God personally and uniquely created you. The text I use here is a personal paraphrase of this passage, crafted by drawing from three versions of the psalm: the Amplified Bible, Young's Literal Translation, and The Readable Bible. My aim is to help you grasp the nuances of the Hebrew language and appreciate the intricate way God formed you:

Verse 13

For You, LORD God, formed and possessed (owned and chose) my innermost/inward parts, my reins. You (wove me) knit me [together] in my mother's womb.

Verse 14

I will give thanks and praise to You (Lord) because I am fearfully (causing respect and reverence of God) and wonderfully [distinguished (crafted to be differentiated and unique)] made; Wonderful are Your marvelous works, And my soul knows it very well (that I need to depend on you).

Verse 15

My substance/frame/ bones/structure was not hidden from You, when I was being formed and made intricately and skillfully woven/formed [as if embroidered with many colors in the womb] in the secret depths of the earth.

Verse 16

Your eyes have seen my unformed substance, and in Your book, everything was written down, all the days that were ordained/appointed/formed for me, when as yet there was not one of them [even taking shape].

Verse 17

How precious also are Your thoughts (words, promises to and) about me, O God! How great and vast is the sum of them!

Verse 18

If I could count them (and I do recount them)! They outnumber the sand. When I awake, I am still with You.

This perspective on God's preparation of the soil of your heart is crucial for understanding why He remains personally involved in your ongoing growth as His child. I will unpack these verses to help you know how integral you are to His plan for this generation. As the apostle Paul proclaimed to the philosophers in Athens:

> *From one man, he made every nation of men, to inhabit all the face of the earth. And he determined their allotted periods in history and the boundaries of their lands. God did this so that they should seek him, and perhaps feel their way toward him and find him, though he is not far from each one of us. As some of your own poets have said, "For in him we live and move and have our being," and "We are also his offspring"* (Acts 17:26–28).

Paul explains that God, the Creator of the universe, not only orchestrates the creation and timing of each person's existence but also sustains and providentially nurtures the spiritual growth of His children. His careful oversight and design of your life began even before you were conceived. Ephesians 1:4 reveals that God chose all who would believe in Him before the foundation of the world. You were created to be His unique expression of grace to your generation. As I mentioned earlier, Ephesians 2:10 further emphasizes this truth: "For we are his handiwork, created in Christ Jesus for good works, which God prepared in advance, that [you] should walk in them."

This reality should strengthen your faith as you reflect on the fact that God created you for this exact moment in history. He has given you the perfect promises and prepared your soul to be the ideal soil to bear His abundant fruit. He has equipped every one of His children, including you, to accomplish His purposes in this world.

In Psalm 139:13–18, the intricate details of your creation are unveiled. Verse 13 begins by focusing on your innermost being. A literal translation reads, "For you have possessed my reins." The word *reins* refers to the kidneys in Hebrew, which ancient cultures understood as the seat of identity, passion, destiny, and purpose. To say that God possesses your reins is to acknowledge that He holds your deepest motivations, passions, and purpose in His hands. From the very moment of conception, God designed you with intentionality and purpose. The passions, longings, and zeal that drive you are not accidental but divinely hardwired into your being. You are created with a destiny, uniquely crafted to fulfill the plans He has for you.

The place of this imputation was in your mother's womb. In a manner reminiscent of Adam's creation, the God of creation stooped from His throne to oversee the formation of each person. Just as Adam was formed and given life through God's breath, so you were formed in your mother's womb. Later, through your encounter with God's Spirit and belief in Christ Jesus, you received His life and His unique promises to fulfill His purpose for you. God chose the time of your birth, the place, your parents, the family, and even the languages you speak. Yet, He never designed you to violate His Word or will. You are always responsible for your choices and actions. To guide you, He sent His Son Jesus Christ, and gave you His Word and Spirit to lead you into all truth. Even so, you had to choose to receive Him, and you now have the ongoing choice to partake of His divine nature and intentionally grow in Him.

Pause and reflect on this profound insight into your purpose. Since you chose to believe in Christ, you can also see that He first chose you. He created you with a God-glorifying and fruitful plan for your life—one that can only be fulfilled His way, through His divine nature flowing in and through you. Jesus says, "I am the vine; you are the branches. Whoever remains in me, and I in them, that person will bear much fruit; for apart from me you cannot produce anything" (John 15:5). This verse emphasizes the vital role of faith and dependence on God for spiritual growth and the fulfillment of your divine purpose.

Psalm 139:14 reveals that your soul, your innermost being, knows this truth as the eternal reality of life: that God created you with a unique destiny and purpose. Through knowing God, you receive the revelation that He is not only your creator and designer but also your redeemer and sustainer. The only way to fulfill your God-given purpose is by relying on His Spirit to live and love through you. You are astonishingly and marvelously made—designed to glorify God and enjoy Him forever. The more you embrace this truth, the more your soul will overflow with worship and praise!

As Pascal, the renowned philosopher, once said, "There is a God-shaped vacuum in the heart of each man which cannot be satisfied by any created thing but only by God the Creator, made known through Jesus Christ." This quote is a powerful reminder that our deepest longings and desires can only be truly fulfilled by our Creator.

As human beings, we instinctively sense that we have a greater purpose and higher calling than mere existence. God created you not just to survive but to thrive and live an abundant life! Yet it is only in Christ that you can fully realize the purpose He wove into you when He formed you in your mother's womb.

The astonishing development of your life in the hidden place of your mother's womb unfolds under the watchful care of God. Psalm 139:15 reveals that He knits you together, choosing your DNA, establishing your gender, and equipping you with the potential talents, skills, and gifts necessary to fulfill His design for your life. Allow the truth of these verses to settle in your heart and mind that God created every part of your being for His good and glorious purposes.

Many of us, however, may struggle to fully embrace this perspective, feeling like some aspects of our lives fall short of the world's standards. We may also judge some parts of our lives as less than the best. We may view certain physical, emotional, or spiritual traits as flaws or believe that challenges or failures disqualify us from being used by God. These doubts often stem from the enemy's lies and the trap of comparison. When we measure ourselves against the culture's ever-changing ideals or the opinions of others, we risk falling into discouragement or self-rejection.

But the truth is, the lies of the world, Satan, and even our sinful nature cannot negate or destroy God's purposes for our lives. No failure is final. Only God, who created us, truly knows who we are and why we were made. When we see ourselves through His eyes and cling to the promises He has given us, we break free from the limitations of self-doubt and comparison.

Rejecting ourselves or the way God created us is a scheme of the enemy meant to undermine His purposes. However, when we embrace and cultivate God's promises through faith, His empowering presence enables us to produce extraordinary fruitfulness for His glory. By trusting Him, we fulfill the unique purpose for which we were created, bringing honor and praise to the One who designed us with such care.

As we continue reflecting on your creation, Psalm 139:16 reveals that God has written a prophetic script of your life. Each day is providentially planned so that everything He has designed into you can bring His glory and goodness into the world. This aligns with Ephesians 2:10, quoted earlier, which reminds us that we are God's handiwork, uniquely created for the good works He has prepared for us to fulfill.

God's preparation of the soil of your soul began long before you took your first breath. Yet, His work in your development didn't stop there. From your earliest moments, even as you rested in your parent's arms, God began to send you His thoughts (Psalm 139:17–18)—thoughts of love, belonging, and potential. His love has always shone upon you like sunshine on a cloudless day, vast and immeasurable, more numerous than the grains of sand on every shore. Each carries a similar message: You are worthy, you belong to God, and you have a significant purpose in others' lives. Your potential for spiritual growth is limitless, rooted in the divine design and love that formed you.

Even if you didn't experience God's love through your earthly parents, His love for you has never wavered. You may have felt abandoned by those who should have cared for you, but God never leaves His garden unattended. His love for His children is steadfast and unwavering; you are never alone, and He never leaves your side. Psalm 139:1–12 beautifully reveals His constant, attentive care of your life, a comforting reminder of His abiding love:

> *O LORD, You have searched me, and you know me. You know when I sit down and when I get up; you understand my thoughts from afar; you search out my path and my place of rest; you are familiar with all my ways. Even before there is a word on my tongue—look, O LORD, you know it completely. You have hemmed me in, both in front and back; you have laid your hand upon me. Such knowledge is so wonderful— so high I cannot grasp it. Where shall I go to escape from your Spirit? Where can I flee from your presence? If I soar to the heavens, you are there; if I make my bed in Sheol—look! You are there too! If I take flight on the wings of the morning, if I dwell at the end of the sea, even there your hand will lead me, and your right hand will take hold of me. Surely, if I ask the darkness to cover me and the light around me to become night—even the darkness is not dark to you! To you the night is as bright as the day—darkness is like light!*

God communicates His love, joy, peace, grace, and mercy through the gospel, the message of his Son's death, burial, and resurrection. This ultimate demonstration of His love comes alive through the effectual call of God, a powerful and irresistible invitation to salvation by the Holy Spirit. Through the revelation of His glory, excellence, divine attributes, and goodness, you receive His magnificent and precious promises. By faith in His truth, you are rescued from the domain of darkness and transferred into the kingdom of His beloved Son. Like carefully prepared soil, your heart is ready to receive the living seed of His promises, designed to fulfill his will. These divine thoughts—seeds of life—are meant to grow in you, restoring His garden of grace in this world and bringing transformation and renewal.

Yet, this is where many struggle to trust God. You are uniquely made, and the words of hope you receive are uniquely given. To cultivate these promises, you must follow the leading of God's Spirit. He sent these promises to guide you, as Psalm 119:105 declares, "Your word is a lamp to guide my feet, a light on my path" (Psalm 119:105). In obedience to His promises, Peter encourages us to add to our faith moral excellence, knowledge, self-control, endurance, godliness, mutual affection, and love (2 Peter 1:5–7). Without "these qualities" (2 Peter 1:8) increasing, he warns, we become "blind—nearsighted" (2 Peter 1:9), blind to the reality that the Spirit gave these precious promises to lift our minds toward "things above" (Colossians 3:2), and "nearsighted" because we focus on ourselves or others instead of Jesus. To see clearly, you must discipline your mind to use His promises as the lens through which you view life, intentionally and continually "fixing [y]our eyes on Jesus, the author, and perfector of [y]our faith" (Hebrews 12:2).

When these precious promises are ingrafted into the soil of your soul and cultivated through abiding meditation, they will produce the image of God's Son in you, revealing His glory to the world. David captures this truth when he exclaims, "I will praise you, because I am fearfully and wonderfully made. Your works are marvelous, and my soul knows it very well" (Psalm 139:14).

What essential attitudes must you adopt to allow the magnificent promises to become a light on your path? The next chapter will explore biblical attitudes such as humility, faith, and perseverance—qualities that nurture your spiritual growth.

CHAPTER 6

KEY ATTITUDES AND INSIGHTS OF AN OPTIMAL DISCIPLE

*My son, if you accept my words and store up
my commandments within you—
applying your ear to wisdom, inclining your heart to understanding.*
PROVERBS 2:1-2

In the previous chapter, we explored the concept of spiritual preparation and how Father God, the Gardener of the True Vine, eagerly prepares our souls to receive His precious seeds, His majestic promises. This preparation, like the nurturing of soil, reveals that He has designed and equipped us to do His will. As we discussed in the previous chapter, Ephesians 2:10 promises, "For we are his handiwork, created in Christ Jesus for good works, which God prepared in advance, that we should walk in them."

God has prepared you to receive His precious promises, but we must accept them and implant them into our hearts. James 1:21 encourages you to "humbly receive the word implanted in you, which can save your souls." Each promise you receive has been lovingly sowed into you to reveal both who He is and who you are. These promises are the perfect seeds for the soil of your soul. Yet, you still have a choice to cultivate each promise with humility so that they grow optimally in your heart. Cultivating your promises is your role in cooperating with His Spirit to become all He purposes you to be. God is faithful to sow the perfect seeds into your soul to grow Christ's character in you. However, unless you surrender to Him and learn to cultivate the garden of your heart by cooperating with

His Spirit, you will never fully realize the potential of your relationship with Jesus.

Cultivating these promises is critical. It requires you to love the truth and walk in obedient faith, accepting and believing fundamental truths about God and yourself. Paul writes in Galatians 5 that God wants you to produce the fruit of the Spirit, while Peter writes in 2 Peter 1:5–7 that you are to add to your faith the qualities of moral excellence, knowledge, self-control, endurance, godliness, mutual affection, and love. As mentioned earlier, "whoever does not have these qualities is blind—nearsighted, having forgotten that they received purification from their past sins." If your life is not producing God's fruit, there is only one option: turn to Jesus and repent.

When Jesus began His ministry, His first message was, "Repent, for the kingdom of heaven has drawn near" (Matthew 4:17). At this very moment in your life, the kingdom of heaven has drawn near, and the Holy Spirit is calling you into a deeper relationship with God. To respond, you must change your thinking and behaviors to align with the reality of the new covenant and the kingdom of heaven in which you dwell. Repentance means turning towards God and away from your previous path. If you are to become optimal in your relationship with Christ, you must continually turn away from the thinking and behaviors influenced by the world, the flesh, and the devil.

Scripture reminds us, "All have sinned and fall short of the glory of God" (Romans 3:23). Sin is defined as missing the mark. When we fail to think, act, or be as Christ created us to be, we experience a lack of abundant life, a sense of loss, and that feeling of "missing the mark." From the moment of your biological birth as a child of Adam, you existed in a state of spiritual death, separated from God and His purposes. Even after being born again into God's kingdom and transferred from the domain of darkness into his glorious light, the false narratives and rebellious behavior do not immediately fall away. Your sinless state will not be realized until Christ takes you home and you receive your new spiritual body. Each person who receives Jesus as their Savior receives salvation at that time, and one day will experience the complete salvation of God. This progressive journey of discipleship is about becoming an optimal disciple as you learn to think and behave more like the citizen of God's kingdom you already are.

Seven Essential Attitudes and Insights

The following are seven essential attitudes and insights that every optimal disciple should strive to embrace. An essential attitude is a critical perspective that allows the Holy Spirit to guide you into deeper trust, faith, and surrender to Jesus Christ. I call these *essential* attitudes and insights because, without them, you will resist the Holy Spirit's guidance and miss the joy of God's work in the garden of your heart as He produces fruit that glorifies Him.

It's important to remember that no one consistently, perfectly, and obediently lives out all these attitudes at all times. Even the apostle Paul writes in Romans 7:18–20:

> *For I know that nothing good dwells in me—that is, in my sinful nature. For the willingness to do good is present in me, but not doing of the good. For I don't do the good I want to do, but I do the very evil I don't want to do. Now if I do what I don't want to do, it is no longer me doing it, but sin that dwells in me that does it.*

As you reflect on this list, know that by humbling yourself before Christ and His Word, He will provide the grace you need to transform your mind. This list highlights the foundational attitudes an optimal disciple asks the Holy Spirit to cultivate in their heart:

1. **God is God; you are not.** "You shall have no other gods before me" (Exodus 20:3).
2. **Romans 8:26–30 reflects *God's agenda* for all who trust Jesus Christ as their Savior.**
3. **Humbly acknowledge that you often lack the discernment to know what God calls *good or evil* in any given situation.** Through engagement with God's Word, you will develop the ability to discern good from evil (Hebrews 5:11–14).

4. **Understand that truth leads to virtue, and virtue leads to freedom.** The disciplines of truth in your life fosters virtue, which is the pathway to true freedom (John 8:32).
5. **Recognize that you are in a spiritual battle and must guard against the devil's schemes.** "Finally, be strong in the Lord and in his mighty power. Put on the full armor of God so that you can stand against the devil's scheme. For we do not wrestle against flesh and blood but against the rulers, against the cosmic powers of this world's darkness, against the authorities, and against the evil spiritual forces in the heavenly realms" (Ephesians 6:10–12). Through selfish pride, you give the enemy access. Judging and comparing yourself to others are tools of the enemy that derail your progress in Christ. Instead, look only to Christ as your standard (2 Corinthians 10:12).
6. **Since you are in Christ, you are already in God's kingdom.** Psalm 23 reveals this present reality: the Shepherd is actively at work in your life right now. This psalm is not merely a comforting truth but an invitation to embrace and live in its reality by faith, allowing God to align your heart and mind with His truth.
7. **Forgiveness is a command, not an option.** If you desire forgiveness, you must choose to forgive. If you seek mercy, you must choose mercy. Forgiveness is a weighty command with the power to transform your life and the lives of others (Matthew 5:7; 6:14–15).

1. God is God; you are not.

God spoke the first commandment simply, "You shall have no other gods before me." The way you demonstrate that you believe God is God, that you are not, and that He is first in your life is revealed by how you regard the Bible. A faithful follower of Jesus Christ loves His Word. We are called to receive and believe the Word of God. Whenever people begin to personally accept Scripture as God's Word spoken to them, they open their hearts and minds, allowing the Holy Spirit to increase their faith and desire to become Christlike.

This growth in faith is beautifully illustrated in Paul's first letter to the church in Thessalonica. Paul commended their remarkable behavior, writing, "You became an example to all the believers in Macedonia and in Achaia. The word of the Lord has rung out from you, not only there but also in every place where news of your faith toward God has spread, such that we have no need to say anything about it" (1 Thessalonians 1:7–8). Paul had nothing to correct or criticize about their faith in Christ. Instead, he gave them glowing praise: *You are doing fantastic—keep doing what you are doing!* This level of faith in God's Word was a glowing report about a new believing congregation. For a young church, their faith in God's Word was extraordinary.

What set the Thessalonian church apart?

Paul reveals that they held an extraordinary trust in God and His Word. He writes in 1 Thessalonians 2:13, "We constantly thank God because of this: that when you received the word of God that you heard from us, you accepted it not as the word of men, but as **what it really is, the word of God,** (which is at work in you believers)" (emphasis mine).

Reverence for God and His Word is the most foundational and powerful of all the essential attitudes and insights of an optimal disciple: *Scripture is God speaking to you.* The Bible is not just another book or source of truth. It is unique because it reveals who Jesus Christ is—that He is "the way and the truth, and the life. No one comes to the Father except through me" (John 14:6).

If you have not humbled your heart and submitted your mind to God and his Word, you will find yourself constantly judging God and His message to you. This critical attitude of judgment prevents you from fully embracing faith and becoming optimal in your walk with Christ. Paul makes it clear that "faith comes from hearing and hearing through the message of Christ" (Romans 10:17).

The independent life inherited from Adam is steeped in innate pride and has already revealed itself as an empty way of life. Faith in Christ's promises, however, allows you to partake in His life, and this requires trust in His Word.

When you settle the matter in your heart that the Scripture is truly God's Word, not merely the word of man, you open yourself to the Holy Spirit. As you read Scripture, the Holy Spirit reads your heart. This attitude of humility and reverence—fear of the Lord—is the beginning of a deeper knowledge of God and the Lord Jesus Christ. Only with this foundational attitude can you grasp the other essential attitudes and insights critical for Christ to lead you into all truth and to become optimal in your relationship with Him.

2. Romans 8:26–30 reflects *God's agenda* for all who trust Jesus Christ as their Savior.
The optimal disciple must grasp the eternal, overarching purposes of God. Understanding God's focuses in your life empowers you to surrender to His will. The Holy Spirit reminds us to "watch carefully as to how you live, not as unwise but as wise, making the most of the time, because the days are evil. Therefore, do not be foolish, but understand what the Lord's will is" (Ephesians 5:15–17).

It is exceedingly difficult to cooperate with God if you have no idea what His agenda is for your life. God expects you to access His Word and know His will and ways. Romans 8:26–30 reveals God's overarching plan for every circumstance you face. These verses make His grand design clear to everyone who trusts Jesus Christ as Savior and Lord:

> *In the same way, the Holy Spirit helps us in our weakness. For we don't know what we ought to pray for, but the Holy Spirit himself intercedes for us with inexpressible groans. And he who searches our hearts knows what the mind of the Holy Spirit is, because the Holy Spirit intercedes for the saints in accordance with the will of God. And we know that God works all things together for good for those who love him, for those who are called according to his purpose; for those he foreknew he also predestined to be conformed to the image of his Son, so that his Son would be the firstborn among many brothers and sisters. And those he predestined he also called; those he called he also justified; and those he justified he also glorified.*

This passage emphasizes that the Holy Spirit "helps us in our weakness" when we don't know what to do or even how to pray. This reminder points to our need to depend on God with a humble heart. Whenever you seek His wisdom in life's circumstances, remember His agenda for you as outlined in these verses. If you love God and trust Jesus Christ for your eternal future, you are on this path in every situation. The ultimate goal of God's agenda for you is to be conformed to and transformed into the likeness of His Son, Jesus Christ.

This has been God's design from the beginning of creation, when "God said, 'Let us make humans in our own image, in our own likeness . . . . So God created humankind in his own image. In the image of God he created them. And he created them male and female." (Genesis 1:26–27) Sadly, Adam and Eve rebelled against God's plan, believing Satan's lies, and shattered the image and likeness of God in humanity.

Yet all who trust in Jesus Christ are being remade into a new creation. As Scripture says, "If anyone is in Christ, they are a new creation" (2 Corinthians 5:17). This is—and always has been—God's agenda for your life. Becoming a faithful follower of Christ often involves walking through dark valleys and overcoming insurmountable obstacles. It requires accepting that God prioritizes your eternal life over your temporary comfort:

> *Jesus said to his disciples, "If anyone wants to come after me, they must deny themselves, take up their cross, and follow me. For whoever wants to save their life will lose it, but whoever loses their life for my sake will find it. For how does a person benefit if they gain the whole world yet lose their soul? What can a person give to God in exchange for their soul?"* (Matthew 16:24–26).

3. Humbly acknowledge that you often lack the discernment to know what God calls *good or evil* in any given situation.

Romans 8:28 reminds us that God's "good" is working everything together in your life for your ultimate good: conforming you to the image of His Son. This process may not always feel like all God's decisions are "good" choices for you. Trust Him—they are.

King David's beloved Psalm 23 says that God leads us into green pastures. This is a fundamental truth about how God always leads. However, the places we end up, even after praying and trusting His promises, may not look or feel "good." Romans 8:28–29 and many other passages affirm this truth.

Consider these examples of "good" that didn't initially appear good:

- **God led Israel to the edge of the Red Sea.** They thought they would die at Pharaoh's hand, yet the sea became God's means of delivering Israel and destroying their enemies (Exodus 14).
- **God led Jesus into the wilderness to be tempted by Satan (Matthew 4:1).** Unless Jesus was tempted as we are, He could not serve as our great High Priest or defeat Satan's hold over the world.
- **The disciples followed Jesus for three years, believing he was God's promised Messiah and the King of Israel.** Yet, on the cross, He suffered and died. For two days, they thought it was the end. But through His death, burial, and resurrection, believers receive eternal life. We now call that day "Good Friday," though at the time, it seemed to be the worst day of their lives.

You face days when your circumstances seem evil rather than good. However, if you trust God through them and ask for His wisdom, you will experience His peace. This is why 1 Thessalonians 5:16–18 commands us:

- "Rejoice always.
- Pray without ceasing.
- Give thanks in everything, for this is God's will for you in Christ Jesus."

These are not lovely little Christian clichés. These are commands of God to keep you in harmony with Him as you are being conformed to His Son's character! Even a cursory reading of Old Testament history reveals that God was never pleased when Israel grumbled and complained about His leadership over them. Grumbling, complaining, and unthankful hearts grieve God's Spirit. You will suffer more than God desires for you simply because of your unbelief of His agenda. Repent! Learn to give thanks continually because in every circumstance, pain, suffering, and joy, your heavenly Father is leading you into green pastures to prepare you to enjoy His kingdom here, and one day in heaven.

How can you yield more to God's Spirit and see His goodness in every circumstance?

The writer of Hebrews offers insight for growing in discernment. He addresses followers of Jesus who struggled to mature spiritually in Hebrews 5:11–14:

> *We have much to say about this, and it is difficult to explain to you because you have become lazy listeners. In fact, by this time you ought to be teachers, but you need someone to teach you again the basic principles of God's word. You have become those who need milk, not solid food! Anyone who lives on milk is unskilled in the righteous word. Indeed, that person is an infant. But solid food is for the mature, for those who by constant use have trained their power of discernment to distinguish between good and evil.*

"Constant use" refers to disciplined thinking and behavior as you trust God's Word.

A practical example of this discipline is "giving thanks" in all circumstances. This simple yet profound act demonstrates obedience and positions you to receive God's wisdom.

Discernment also requires understanding that humanity is infected with a terminal disease called sin, inherited from Adam. Adam and Eve's disobedience—choosing to eat from the Tree of Knowledge of Good and Evil—introduced a bias towards sin into all humanity. Sin deceives us into thinking we know what is "good" and "evil." Abandoning this false narrative is essential for walking with God's Spirit.

Right and wrong are generally clear through God's commandments, such as the Ten Commandments and Jesus' teachings in the Sermon on the Mount. These principles act as road signs and boundaries to keep us on the right path. However, discernment is required when circumstances challenge these boundaries.

Consider this example: If my wife were experiencing a medical emergency, I would exceed the speed limit or even drive outside the road's boundaries to get her to the hospital. This decision may break traffic laws, but saving her life would align with what is good in God's eyes. Similarly, Scripture provides examples of breaking one commandment to uphold a higher one, such as when the Jewish midwives *lied* to save Hebrew babies from Pharaoh's decree (Exodus 1:15–21).

Through constant study of God's Word and the guidance of His Spirit, you can learn to discern what is good and evil in God's eyes. The key to this discernment is maintaining a humble attitude, being willing to second-guess yourself rather than God. Trust that every circumstance, no matter how challenging, is part of His plan to conform you to the image of Christ. When faced with uncomfortable circumstances, give thanks and humbly yield to God, knowing He works all things together for the good of those who love Him.

4. Understand that truth leads to virtue, and virtue leads to freedom. This essential attitude—that the spiritual discipline of following the truth leads to freedom, is often undermined by worldly, temporal thinking.

- My best definition of spiritual discipline is *any <u>repeated</u> mental, emotional, or physical activity through which one partakes of or participates in the divine nature through God's promises to glorify Him.*
- The discipline of truth involves repeated actions or courses of action that, over time, create space for the Holy Spirit to transform your inner being through your obedience. These promises form the character of Christ in you. For example, "Blessed are the merciful, for they will receive mercy" (Matthew 5:7), or, "Give, and it will be given to you, the full measure (i.e., pressed down, shaken together, and flowing over). They will pour it into your lap, for by your standard of measure it will be measured back to you" (Luke 6:38).

Human nature often falsely equates intellectually agreeing with the truth to living out and experiencing the transforming wisdom of *the* truth. However, God's desire is not for you to simply accomplish a task for Him but to become conformed to the image of His Son. This transformation into Christlikeness requires disciplined change and a consistent practice of believing and living out the truth.

The transformation of a crawling caterpillar into a beautiful butterfly illustrates the role of discipline in achieving a new creation. The caterpillar must remain in the cocoon until it becomes a butterfly. Compared to the butterfly, the caterpillar has little freedom, but gaining the freedom to fly requires enduring the restricted discipline of the cocoon until its transformation is complete. The process cannot be hurried or avoided.

The truth that discipline develops virtue is embraced and celebrated in the heart of every optimal disciple. Jesus made this connection between truth and freedom when he tells a group of believing Jews, "If you remain [abide] in my word, you are truly my disciples. Then you will know the truth, and the truth will set you free" (John 8:31–32, addition mine). Remaining or abiding in Him and His Word gives you the freedom from sin and the grace to do God's will.

If you walk in the discipline of abiding in Christ and His promises, your boldness in prayer will increase as your desire to glorify God increases. Glorifying God is a critical condition for fruitful prayers. Jesus teaches this truth to His disciples on the night He was betrayed:

> *I'm telling you the truth: Anyone who believes in me will do the works I have done, and they'll do greater works than these, because I'm going to the Father. And whatever you ask in my name, I will do it so that the Father may be glorified through the works of the Son. If you ask me for anything in my name, I will do it* (John 14:12–13).

Closely following Jesus will inevitably involve sacrifice and suffering. Yet, the optimal disciple embraces this with joy because:

> *We rejoice in our sufferings, knowing that suffering produces perseverance, perseverance produces proven character, and proven character produces hope. And hope does not disappoint, because God's love has been poured into our hearts through the Holy Spirit, who has been given to us* (Romans 5:3-5).

Failure to live out an optimal commitment to Jesus is always a matter of discipline. However, discipline fueled by pride or self-will cannot bear lasting fruit. All fruitful discipline must stem from a love of Christ and a desire to create space for the Holy Spirit to work in your heart.

Earlier in this book, I pointed out how New Testament believers are repeatedly warned and encouraged to remain faithful to the promises they first believed about Jesus. Renewing your commitment to your first love and initial convictions creates a foundation for transforming convictions. Through these promises, you partake of Christ's divine nature. However, if you grow lax in intentionally hungering and thirsting for Him through your spiritual disciplines, you will slow down the process of becoming the optimal disciple He designed you to be.

5. Recognize that you are in a spiritual battle and must guard against the devil's schemes. The apostle Paul boldly gives this powerful warning to the Ephesian church:

> *Finally, be strong in the Lord and in his mighty power. Put on the full armor of God so that you can stand against the devil's schemes. For we do not wrestle against flesh and blood but against the rulers, against the cosmic powers of this world's darkness, against the authorities, and against the evil spiritual forces in the heavenly realms*
> (Ephesians 6:10–12).

This warning remains accurate and essential for any disciple seeking to glorify Christ. You must be disciplined to avoid Satan's traps and schemes to become the optimal disciple God desires you to be. A key to this battle is understanding his lies and how he appeals to your selfish pride. It is through selfish pride that Satan gains access to your heart. To guard against his schemes, you must discipline your mind and heart to avoid at least three key traps, which can pull you into the whirlpool of wickedness.

a. Walk in the counsel of God's Word and God's people.

Psalm 1:1 says the blessed person does not "walk in the counsel of the wicked." Instead, the optimal disciple walks in the counsel of God's Word and in fellowship with honorable people who seek Him. Pride often tempts us to wrestle with others (flesh and blood), but forgiveness, forbearance, and humility maintain the unity of the Spirit and the bond of peace. Angry and contentious people easily fall right into Satan's traps.

Your deepest friendships should be with men and women of integrity who love the Lord Jesus. The writer of Hebrews emphasizes this repeatedly, encouraging Jewish believers to remain steadfast in their faith in Christ:

> *Take care, brothers and sisters, that there never be in any of you an evil, unbelieving heart that leads you to fall away from the living God. Rather, encourage one another daily, as long as it is called "today" so that none of you will be hardened by the deceitfulness of sin. For we have become participants in the life of Christ if indeed we hold firmly to our original conviction till the end* (Hebrews 3:12–14).

Fellowship with godly people allows you to partake of the divine nature through their encouragement and example. This does not mean we avoid associating with ungodly people, but it does mean you should not seek their counsel or allow their advice to shape your decisions.

b. Stand faithfully in the ways of God.

Psalm 1:1 also declares that the blessed person does not "stand in the way of sinners." Instead, the optimal disciple stands firmly in God's ways, knowing they lead to life. As expressed in Psalm 86:11–12, "O Lord, teach me your ways that I may walk in your truth; unite my divided heart to fear your name. O Lord my God, I will praise you with all my heart, and I will glorify your name forevermore." The optimal disciple resolves to follow Jesus with no turning back. Standing firm in Christ is not about achieving perfection but about "fixing our eyes on Jesus, the author and perfecter of our faith" (Hebrews 12:2).

c. Avoid sitting in a seat with scoffers.

Psalm 1:1 warns against "sit[ting] in a seat with scoffers." This refers to the temptation to judge or compare yourself to others. The optimal disciple seeks to encourage others rather than look down on them. Judging others often comes through the lens of legalism, where pride leads us to elevate ourselves or disqualify ourselves from our God-given responsibilities. Paul warns in 2 Corinthians 10:12, "We do not dare to classify or compare ourselves with some who commend themselves. For when they measure themselves by themselves and compare themselves with themselves, they do not see clearly." The only standard for comparison is Jesus Christ. Humility before God allows you to discover your identity, righteousness, and value in Him.

Humility before God is essential for resisting the devil. Scripture consistently proclaims, "God opposes the proud but shows favor to the humble" (James 4:6). Pride is the tool Satan uses to convince you that you can control your life by demanding your own "good." As C. S. Lewis wrote in *Mere Christianity*, "Pride is spiritual cancer: it eats up the very possibility of love, or contentment, or even common sense." Through humility and dependence on God, you can guard against Satan's schemes, resist his lies, and walk in the freedom and victory of Christ.

6. Since you are in Christ, you are already in God's kingdom.
King David is credited with the writing of Psalm 23, but God is the true author. Every phrase and every word reveals who God is and what He is actively doing in your life:

> *The LORD is my shepherd; I shall not want. He makes me lie down in green pastures; he leads me beside still waters; he restores my soul; he leads me in paths of righteousness for his name's sake. Even though I walk through the valley of the shadow of death, I fear no evil, for you are with me; your rod and your staff, they comfort me; you prepare a table before me in the presence of my enemies; you anoint my head with oil—my cup overflows. Surely goodness and lovingkindness will pursue me all the days of my life, and I shall dwell in the house of the LORD forever* (Psalm 23:1–6).

As you read this psalm, read it in its present tense because that is how it is written. Where are you right now? According to Psalm 23, you are not in need. You are resting in a green pasture. Sheep love green pastures, and they drink only from still waters. Spiritually, this is where you always are, through faith, in God's kingdom.

You might say, "I don't *feel* like this describes my present circumstances." That is when you need to accept, embrace, and give thanks to God so that He can open your eyes to the reality of where you truly are. Psalm 23 is a place of rest. If you trust in Him and lean into the promises He has given you, you will find rest for your soul.

The key attitude to cultivate is recognizing that rest, like peace, is not controlled by your material or physical circumstances. Rest, peace, calm assurance, and contentment are attitudes of faith in your heavenly Father.

Mentally and emotionally, walk through each verse of this psalm, allowing it to define who and where you are. As you surrender to His truth, you will be amazed by the deep peace and overwhelming gratitude that will flood your heart and mind.

7. Forgiveness is a command, not an option.
If you want to be forgiven, you must choose forgiveness; if you want mercy, you must choose mercy. The Scriptures are clear and direct about forgiveness: "Blessed are the merciful, for they will receive mercy" (Matthew 5:7). Jesus amplifies this truth in Matthew 6:14–15, "If you forgive others for their sins, your heavenly Father will also forgive you. But if you don't forgive others for their sins, your Father will not forgive your sins."

The optimal disciple follows the Shepherd closely, modeling the compassion of Jesus Christ. Choosing not to forgive is an act of raw rebellion against the basic principles of the King and His kingdom. Our hearts should continually cry out for mercy and forgiveness, not just for ourselves but also for others.

This list does not provide an exhaustive account of every essential attitude an optimal disciple must have because, like you, I am still growing in faith in Christ. Every optimal disciple is a teachable learner, humbled before God's revealed Word. However, I know, based on the authority of Scripture, that each of these attitudes listed above is essential to staying obedient to the Holy Spirit's work of conforming you to the image of Christ.

I hope this chapter gave you insight into what God is doing and why He allows you to face struggles. The problems you encounter are never the most significant problem. The greatest challenge in every trial is whether you will trust God in and through it. Without embracing these seven attitudes (expect God to teach you additional ones), you will continually chafe under the yoke of His promises, which are given to conform you to the likeness of His Son.

There are essential questions to ask yourself in every trial, blessing, and moment to remain close to Jesus:

- Am I choosing to believe God, and am I humbling myself before Him?
- Am I walking in the light of God's revealed will for me?
- Am I seeking God's wisdom in each challenge?
- Do I trust God, His Word, and his Spirit to accomplish what He promises?
- Am I continuing the spiritual disciplines that empower me to partake of the divine nature of Christ?

To trust God and follow Him through life's struggles requires faith. The faith you need comes through believing the promises of God revealed in Christ. His message of promise reaches your heart as you hear His voice, knowing that "faith comes by hearing and hearing through the message of Christ" (Romans 10:17).

Psalm 84 beautifully expresses the essential attitudes of the optimal disciple. It is the song of every heart that longs to finish strong in the Lord:

> *How lovely is your dwelling place, O LORD of Armies! My soul yearns, even faints, to be in the courts of the LORD; my heart and my flesh cry out for the living God. Even the sparrow has found a home, and the swallow has a nest for herself where she may lay her young near your altars, O LORD of Armies, my King, and my God. Blessed are those who dwell in your house, ever praising you. Blessed are those whose strength is in you, whose hearts are set on the pathways to Jerusalem, who make the Valley of Weeping a place of springs when they pass through it. (Like the autumn rain that covers the valley with blessings), who go from strength to strength until every one of them appears before God in Zion. O LORD God of Armies, hear my prayer; listen, O God of Jacob; look at our shield, O*

God; look upon the face of your anointed. For a day in your courts is better than a thousand elsewhere. I would rather be a doorkeeper in the house of my God than dwell in the tents of the wicked. For the Lord *God is a sun and shield; the* Lord *gives grace and glory; he withholds no good thing from those who walk uprightly. O* Lord *of Armies, blessed is the one who trusts in you.*

Chapter 7 will explore *how* Christ is, and has been, discipling you through His Spirit and Word. It will also explain *how you can partake of His* promises, allowing them to become a lamp to your feet and a light to your path. How do you cultivate your unique precious promises? How do meditation and abiding in Christ empower you to grow in grace? These are the questions we will delve into in the next chapter.

CHAPTER 7

How Do the Magnificent and Precious Promises Become a Light to Your Path?

God took [Abram] outside and said, "Look toward the heavens and count the stars—if you are able to count them." Then He said to him, "That's how many descendants you will have." Abram believed the Lord, so he counted him as righteous."
GENESIS 15:5

Why does God make personal promises to you? The short answer, found in 2 Peter 1:4, is "so that through them you may become partakers of the divine nature." The personalized promises He gives you are the optimal, deeply personal way for you to know God and fulfill His will in this world. Through God's personal, loving messages, you are conformed and transformed into the image and identity of His Son, Jesus Christ.

In this chapter, you will begin to understand the ***process*** by which Christ is—and *has been*—discipling you. As you come to recognize this process in your life, you can yield more fully to Christ's Spirit, leading to greater spiritual fruitfulness. The word *process* refers to a systematic series of actions directed towards a specific goal. That goal is your transformation into the image and identity of God's Son. These systematic actions are as organic as a seed growing into a plant that produces fruit—or as powerful as a seed lodged in a crevasse, growing into a tree that eventually splits the solid rock. Remember, God's power within you is the infusion of eternal life as you partake of the divine nature! This life is far more than the biological life received through Adam; it is the life of God at work in you.

The more you understand God's transformative processes and the ways His great and precious promises work in your heart, the more empowered you are to follow His Spirit wholeheartedly. To gain deeper insight, consider the metaphors the Bible uses to describe His Word.

The Bible Speaks of His Promises through Various Metaphors

Reflect on the following verses to grasp why and how the promises of God's Word, given to you through His Spirit, possess power to transform your life:

1. His Word is like seed—alive and capable of producing spiritual growth.

- Jesus said in the parable of the Sower, "The seed is the word of God" (Luke 8:11).
- Peter echoes this metaphor in 1 Peter 1:23, "For you have been born again, not of perishable seed, but of imperishable, through the living and enduring word of God."
- James encourages us to "humbly receive the word implanted in you, which can save your souls" (James 1:21).
- Psalm 1:3 declares that we are to become "like a tree planted by the streams of water that yields it fruit in season."

2. His Word has the power to clean, prune, and judge.

- Paul writes in Ephesians 5:25, "Husbands, love your wives just as Christ loved the church and gave himself up for her, that he might make her holy, cleansing her by the washing of the water by God's word."

- In John 15, Jesus teaches that we are branches in Him, the true vine. He says in verse 3, "You are already cleaned because of the word I have spoken to you."
- Hebrews 4:12: "For the word of God is living and active, sharper than any double-edged sword, piercing as far as the division of soul and of spirit, and of joints and of marrow, able to judge the thoughts and attitudes of the heart."

3. The Word is Christ in you:

- John 1:14 tells us, "The Word became flesh and lived among us."
- 1 Thessalonians 2:13: "We constantly thank God because of this: that when you received the word of God that you heard from us, you accepted it not as the word of men, but as what it really is, the word of God, (which is at work in you believers)."
- Colossians 3:16: "Let the word of Christ richly dwell within you."

It's vital to internalize the truths behind these metaphors. When you receive God's Word, promise, or seed, you're not merely receiving a concept. You are receiving the living, active Word—Jesus, the incarnate Son of God. This revelation is uniquely personal to each of us, making our faith journey profoundly meaningful.

In his second epistle, Peter explains that God's messages and promises are revealed as we experience the glory of Jesus Christ. His promises are unveiled when we experience His glory and virtue. In these moments, Jesus implants His promises in our hearts like seeds, designed to grow and produce His life within us—just as a natural seed grows in soil to reproduce its life. As the character of Christ develops within us, the living Word works in us, washing, cleansing, and pruning us from the filth of this world, transforming us into His divine nature. This transformation is both powerful and hope-filled, encouraging us to continue on our spiritual journey.

As mentioned, we often experience Christ's glory and goodness in moments of vulnerability and need. However, we also encounter His glory and virtue in times of extreme blessing and joy, when we celebrate His goodness with gratitude and thanksgiving. In every circumstance, one truth remains constant: God's grace is always extended to the humble, those with hearts like soft, fertile soil, ready to receive and nurture His promises.

What Did You Do with Your Seeds/Promises?

When God gives a promise, we often see it as a momentary gift to meet a need, relieve pain, heal a wound, or reveal His love, prompting praise and worship. We may approach God seeking relief from our circumstances, and He graciously answers. However, His promises are never intended to simply provide temporary relief, allowing us to return to unchanged, untransformed lives.

God's magnificent and precious promises are like seeds. While natural seeds can be consumed for sustenance, their greater purpose is to be planted, bloom, bear fruit, and produce even more seeds, transforming the world around them. In the same way, God's promises are meant to bring life and transformation.

You must accept that spiritual fruit cannot be produced through your willpower. If you desire the fruit of the Spirit, you must surrender to the Spirit of God and embrace His promises as living truth. When trusted and cultivated, these personalized promises will produce their own fruitful life within you, bringing spiritual rest and renewal to your soul.

How I Experienced the Process

It took me years to understand how God was forming His life in me. Comprehending His ways is part of my story and demonstrates His gracious patience in developing His image and character in me. As I shared in the introduction, I confessed my faith in Jesus Christ in 1970 at the age of 19. My greatest obstacle to trusting Jesus as my Savior was my unbelief that Jesus Christ is the Son of God who came in the flesh. Before I could place my faith in Christ, I humbled myself before God and asked this question, **"God, is the man Jesus Christ truly Your Son?"**

This truth is essential for genuine faith and a biblical relationship with God. As John's Gospel tell us, it is the way to become a child of God:

> *Yet to all who did receive him, to those who believed in his name, he gave the right to become children of God, born not of human descent, nor of sexual desire, nor of a human's decision, but born of God. The Word became flesh and lived among us. We saw his glory, the glory of the one and only Son from the Father, full of grace and truth* (John 1:12–14).

I cannot fully explain how God revealed this truth to me, but I know it was not through anyone convincing me. It remains a mystery—a moment when belief swept over my heart and mind as I chose to trust. Overnight, I went from a rebellious pagan, determined to have my own way, to a child of God who desired His will and His way. I was filled with joy, confident that I had chosen well because *I had chosen* Him.

My initial testimony and witness to others centered on the joy and peace I experienced in coming to Christ. I would tell people, "You can know God if you choose Jesus Christ as your Savior." My message was that life would be immeasurably better if they made that choice. This approach worked for a week or so, but soon a troubling, weakening thought began to plague me: *Maybe my life changed because I chose Jesus, but what if He did not choose me?* Doubts crept in—what if my decision was merely an emotional response or an act of will on my part? Why would a holy and perfect God want someone like me, anyway?

I can't recall exactly how I came across John 15:16, but I vividly remember the effect it had on my heart and mind. The verse brought me sweet assurance and peace, dispelling my fears. In this verse, Jesus declares to His disciples and to all whom He calls to Himself, "You didn't choose me, but I chose you and appointed you so that you would go and bear fruit, and that your fruit should remain so that the Father will give you whatever you ask for in my name."

Now I Know

In my vulnerable state of doubting God's calling, I now see why the Holy Spirit revealed Jesus' glory and excellence and planted a magnificent and precious promise—a seed of truth—into my heart. That promise met my immediate need, replacing my fears and doubts with renewed faith. I simply ate the precious seed! It brought relief and assurance, confirming that I was chosen by Christ. I resumed my new life in Him, though I did not yet understand the importance of cultivating that promise within my soul.

As my testimony of God's kindness deepened, I shared the good news of salvation through Jesus Christ and the truth of His choosing us. Yet, God was not finished transforming my mind. Through this promise, he continued to shape me, teaching me His ways and drawing me deeper into His truth.

The Seed Truth of Promise Began to Transform Me

Several months later, God used John 15:16 to guide my spiritual journey in a new way. Until that point, I had been using this verse to share the good news of God's love. One day, after sharing my faith and experiencing the joy of leading someone to Christ, God impressed these words on my heart through this passage, "I chose you and *appointed you* so that you would go and bear fruit, and that your fruit should remain" (emphasis mine).

This time, the verse carried a deeper message. God used it to call me into ministry, impressing upon my heart that I was to serve as a pastor and teacher. Once again, I was overwhelmed and broken by His love and gracious kindness. My heart responded with a mixture of joy and fear—joy because of God's unmistakable presence, but fear and reluctance because I had very little confidence in, or respect for, organized religion.

As a former pagan unbeliever, I had developed deep mistrust of religious institutions. In fact, I was so skeptical that I didn't even trust Billy Graham at the time. The thought of being called to lead a church felt overwhelming and unwelcomed.

Yet, this was part of God's design for me, His good works prepared before the foundation of the world (Ephesians 1:4; 2:10). As Psalm 139:13 (KJV) declares, it was He who "possessed my reins" and "covered me in my mother's womb." He chose my DNA, wrote my destiny in His book, prepared the soil of my heart, and orchestrated the events that led me to believe and enter the kingdom of His beloved Son.

But the story of this seed—the promise John 15:16—did not end there. Over the years, I began to connect the dots and understand how the Spirit had been transforming me through the working of the Word and this promise. Now I know it was a promise *personalized* to me by God's Spirit.

Cultivating the Promise

At one point, I became convicted to memorize, study, and meditate on John 15:1–17. After years of cultivating this magnificent promise (seed), it became like an artesian spring of God's grace, love, life, and truth flowing through my soul. He taught me how to abide in Him and His Word. Through this passage, He transformed and renewed my mind, teaching me how His Spirit loves others through me. As Isaiah 55 promises, the Word He planted has borne fruit: I now have seed to sow into others' hearts and spiritual bread to nourish and build up the body of Christ.

The promise of John 15:16 became a garden of grace and truth in my life, revealing Jesus Christ to me and transforming my heart. I now understand that this is not simply an intellectual exercise of believing in truth. It's about cooperating with God's process, participating in His divine nature, and allowing His Spirit to work in and through me.

I could walk you through the Holy Spirit's work in my spiritual formation using passages like Psalm 1; 51; 139; Proverbs 2:1–5; Isaiah 55; Matthew 11:25–30, and many others, much as I illustrated using John 15:1–17. Each of these passages has become a magnificent and precious promise to me—sacred spaces where I daily commune with God and contemplate the beauty of the Lord. I encourage you to ask God to help you discern the promises He has given you so you can begin to intentionally cooperate with His Spirit. The psalmist modeled this in Psalm 119:49 when he prayed "Remember your word to your servant, in which you have made me hope."

My point is this: God intends to use every word and promise He gives us when we humbly encounter His glory and excellence. His purpose is to transform our minds and conform our lives to the image of His Son. His promises are not merely answers to our questions or solutions to our current crises. They are seeds of promise—planted to reveal His kingdom, manifest His grace, and demonstrate His salvation and power through us.

Yet it took me years—marked by failure and stumbling—to understand the connection between His promises and the path I was *providentially* walking. It wasn't until I came to understand the truths in 2 Peter 1 that everything began to make sense. Now, my focus on Christ Jesus and God's Word has become much more intentional. I meditate, abide, cultivate, pray, and seek communion with Christ daily. Through this, I worship God by believing and trusting in the *personalized promises* He has given me. The results have been inspiring, sustaining, fruitful, and restful in Christ. I now see why Peter so strongly encourages us when he writes:

> *For this very reason, make every effort to add to your faith moral excellence; and to moral excellence, knowledge; and to knowledge, self-control; and to self-control, endurance; and to endurance, godliness; and to godliness, mutual affection; and to mutual affection, love. For if these qualities are in you and increasing, they will keep you from being ineffective and unproductive in the knowledge of our Lord Jesus Christ. For whoever does not have these qualities is blind—nearsighted, having forgotten that they received purification from their past sins. So, brothers and sisters, be diligent to make your calling and election firm, for by doing this you will never stumble; and this way you will receive a rich welcome into the eternal kingdom of our Lord and Savior Jesus Christ* (2 Peter 1:5–11).

This Process Is the Skill You Must Develop

As you intentionally focus on the unique and precious promises God has given you, your faith will grow. You must consistently fix your eyes on Jesus, the author and perfecter of your faith. This is not merely an act of observation but a transformative process. You engage in this process by mediating on His Word, abiding in His presence, cultivating His promises in your heart, seeking communion with Christ, and worshiping God by believing and trusting in the promises He has given you.

This is how God intends His personal, precious promises to become a light to your path and a lamp for your feet. The more you focus on God through His promises, the more you will understand your identity in Christ and how He desires to fulfill His Word in your life. This growing understanding is not simply knowledge; it is an active source of empowerment from God's Spirit.

Chapter 8 will take you on a journey through the entire Bible, helping you grasp how God's promises have always been the driving force behind the past and present creation of His kingdom on earth. As you read, pay attention to how God spoke His promises to people, including you, to further His kingdom. You are not a passive reader but an active participant in God's grand plan. Your role is significant, and your actions are part of His divine strategy.

PREFACE TO CHAPTER 8

From one man [God] made every nation of men, to inhabit all the face of the earth. And He determined their allotted periods in history and the boundaries of their lands. God did this so that they would seek him, and perhaps feel their way toward him and find him, though he is not far from each one of us.
ACTS 17:26–27

Throughout the first seven chapters, you have been encouraged to view your spiritual formation through the lens provided in 2 Peter 1. This perspective highlights the personal way God has been guiding you through His promises and special messages—messages that inspire, comfort, and correct your walk with the Holy Spirit. You've learned that as you intentionally cooperate in obedience to partake of the divine nature, you experience spiritual growth.

The next chapter offers a brief overview of how God has always interacted with humanity through His promises. From walking in the garden with Adam, through the history of Israel, to the coming of Christ Jesus and the birth of the church at Pentecost, God's promises have been central. Throughout history, it has been those who believed in God and His promises who carried the good news to reverse the curse of sin and expand His kingdom.

The purpose of this important, albeit longer, chapter is to impress upon your heart that God, the ever-trustworthy One, stands behind His Word, His promises, and His message. He uses these to inspire His followers to fulfill their destiny as the kings and priests He created humanity to be. The Lord is trustworthy; He has always been trustworthy, and He will remain faithful to the great and magnificent promises He has given you.

CHAPTER 8

THE GOD OF YOUR PROMISES

We did not follow cleverly devised tales when we made known to you the power and coming of our Lord Jesus Christ.
2 PETER 1:16

Your great and magnificent promises, given by Jesus Christ when He called you to Himself, are connected to all of God's promises through His unwavering faithfulness. The God revealed in the incarnation of Jesus Christ has always related to humanity through promises (or personalized messages) because He desires to reveal Himself to humankind through a personal, loving relationship. These promises are expressed in Scripture as laws, testimonies, statutes, principles, commands, instructions, judgments, precepts, regulations, and rules. They are also seen in His acts of mercy, which demonstrate His dynamic authority in the creation of His kingdom and the redemption and correction of humanity. All of these reveal God's personal communication with His creation. From the first verses of Genesis, where God speaks worlds into existence, to Revelation 22:7, where Jesus proclaims, "Look, I am coming soon!" the Bible is a record of God's promises. These promises propel the story of His love and care for all humanity. As we partake of His divine nature through the promises we have received from Christ, we are empowered by God's eternal life to be and do all the "good works, which God prepared in advance, that we should walk in them" (Ephesians 2:10).

A brief overview of the Bible reveals how God has always worked through His spoken words, which take the form of promises. The writer of Hebrews declares, "By faith we understand that the universe was *created by the spoken word of God* so that what is seen was not made out of things that were visible" (Hebrews 11:3, emphasis mine). Peter echoes this truth in 2 Peter 3:5, *"By the spoken word of God* long ago the heavens came into being and the earth was formed out of water and by water" (emphasis mine).

Spoken Words: Different yet Congruent

Before you embark on this journey through the Scriptures, I encourage you to read Psalm 119. This psalm is a masterful display of parallel Hebrew poetry, where most verses highlight the Lord's spoken messages. Nearly all of its 176 verses provide a different yet harmonious expression of God's communication to His people.

Here are 12 examples from Psalm 119. Each italicized word (emphasis mine) is unique, yet all are congruent, working together to reveal God's heart and purpose:

- "Blessed are those who keep his *statutes*, who seek him with their whole heart, who also do no wrong, but walk in his *ways*" (vv. 2–3).
- "You have commanded that your *laws* be kept diligently; oh, that my ways were steadfast, always in line with your *statutes*; then I would not be ashamed when I consider all your *commands*" (vv. 4–6).
- "How can a young person keep their way pure? By watching over it according to your *word*" (v. 9).
- "I have rejoiced in living within the boundaries of your *rules* as much as I have rejoiced in all riches" (v. 14).
- "Turn my eyes away from looking at worthless things; restore me to your *path*" (v. 37).
- "May your lovingkindness be my comfort, according to your *promise* to your servant" (v. 76).
- "My eyes fail, searching for your *promise*, asking, 'When will you comfort me?'" (v. 82).
- "I will never forget your *precepts*, for you have given me life through them" (v. 93).

- "The wicked wait to destroy me, but I diligently consider your *testimonies*. I see a limit to all human perfection, but your *commands* are without limit" (v. 95).
- "I have not departed from your *judgments*, for you yourself have taught me" (v. 102).

When God uses any of these words, they flow from His mouth with unity and congruence, each delivering a personalized message to His people. It's a testament to His understanding and care for each of us.

The comprehensive power of all the messages from God's mouth is expressed in Deuteronomy 8:3. The verse quoted from Young's Literal Translation says, "…that not by bread alone doth man live, but by **every produce** *(everything)* of the mouth of Jehovah man doth live." (my emphasis and addition) Among the various terms used to convey His messages, the word "promise" stands out as the most personal. By embracing the personal way God has always related to humanity, we can rejoice in knowing that He stands behind every single one of His spoken messages. His promises are as reliable as He is, making Him the ultimate promise keeper.

As you reflect on the history of God's care for humanity, you should be deeply encouraged. It demonstrates His faithfulness in fulfilling every promise He has made.

Isaiah 55:10–11 beautifully captures the power of God's spoken messages, highlighting their impact on His people, His purposes, and your personal life:

> *For just as the rain and snow come down from the sky and don't return there until they water the earth and make it fruitful and sprout crops, giving seed to the sower and food to the eater, so is my message (my word that goes out from my mouth*) when I speak it.* It will not return to me unsuccessful. *Rather, it will accomplish what I desire and succeed in the matter I sent it* (emphasis mine plus *addition from the NIV).

God's Spoken Word Created the Universe

From the very beginning, God's spoken word shaped the universe. As you reflect on the days of creation, you can see how His word brought order out of chaos. God separated darkness from light and created the lights to govern the day and night. Each day, more of God's intricate design unfolded as He brought living creation into being—all by His spoken word. On the sixth day, His crowning act of creation was humankind, made in His likeness and image. We can be very thankful that all he created by His promises still stands today!

Adam and Eve were created to be co-regents on earth, living in God's paradise and carrying out His plan. To fulfill this role, Adam was entrusted with additional promises, commands, and instructions to expand and steward the garden until it filled the whole earth.

From the very first moments of their creation, God related to Adam and Eve personally, giving them promises in the form of commands. These instructions outlined what they were to do in partnership with Him. If Adam faithfully followed God's commands, they would produce the excellent world and goodness God intended. But God also promised consequences if they chose to reject His word.

The Rejection of God's Word and Promises Brought Evil into the World

Adam and Eve chose to rebel against God, rejecting His authority and the promises of His created order. They discarded His commands and sought to rule creation independently of Him. Adam allowed Satan, in the form of a serpent, to deceive and seduce Eve. After listening to her, Adam ratified their rebellion by eating the forbidden fruit, seeking to become gods themselves. However, instead of achieving independence, they became enslaved to Satan.

By believing and acting on Satan's lies, Adam and Eve realized the devastating truth; rather than gaining autonomy, they had become dependent slaves of sin. Their rebellion against God separated them—and all their descendants—from His eternal life. As a result, all creation was subjected to frustration and futility. Adam's rebellion disrupted the harmony of creation, severing it from the source of life, causing it to wither like a branch cut off from a tree.

Yet, even as God confronted Adam and Eve in their rebellion and sin, He offered a promise of hope for humanity. This promise would serve as a prophecy of restoration, foreshadowing the reversal of the curse they had brought upon God's creation. God declared that He would destroy the power of evil and reclaim authority from the fallen angel. Speaking directly to Satan, the Lord God delivered the first of many restorative and corrective promises, providing a beacon of hope for the future:

> *Because you have done this, you are cursed above all the livestock and all the wild animals. You will crawl on your belly and eat dust all the days of your life. And I will put enmity between you and the woman, and between your descendants and her descendants. One of her descendants will crush your head, and you will bruise his heel* (Genesis 3:15).

All God's Covenants Contain His Promises

Although physical creation continued to exist in the natural order, it remained separated from the eternal life of God. As a result, Adam and Eve's descendants who did not trust God through faith in His promises spiraled further into sin and rebellion. This moral decline reached a point where God's justice and mercy required the destruction of all humanity, except for Noah and his family, who were preserved in an ark.

Wickedness carries consequences, and in His wisdom and love for humanity, God chose to begin His redemptive plan anew through Noah's family. Once again, God declared a restorative promise, revealed through the sign of the rainbow, as reassurance of His commitment to reverse the effects of the fall. The rainbow promise served as guarantee to Noah's descendants that the Lord would never again destroy the earth by flood. In Genesis 8:21–22, God made this promise:

> *Never again will I curse the ground because of people, even though every intent of their heart is evil from their youth. And I will never again wipe out every living creature as*

I have done. As long as the earth remains, seedtime and harvest, cold and heat, summer and winter, and day and night will not cease.

Theologians refer to this as the Noahic Covenant. A covenant is an agreement, contract, or promise between parties. In this covenant, God takes full responsibility for ensuring that the earth will never again be destroyed by water—a promise He has faithfully upheld to this very day.

The next major covenant in history is the one between God and Abram. Through Abram and his family, God began laying the foundation to restore and bless all humanity.

Genesis 12:1–3 records the promises made to Abram:

The LORD said to Abram, "Leave your country, your people, and your father's house, and go to the land that I will show you. I will make you into a great nation, and I will bless you and make your name great. You will be a blessing, and I will bless those who bless you and curse those who curse you. And through you all the peoples on earth will be blessed."

This covenant, known as the Abrahamic Covenant, highlights the personal way God spoke and related to Abram, just as He had spoken to Adam and Noah. God's messages, expressed as promises, laws, instructions, statutes, and commandments were always designed to draw people into a personal relationship with Him, not to create a distance between God and His creation.

This covenant with Abram continued and extended the first promise given in the garden. It was both creative and redemptive, building on God's pledge to reverse the death, separation, and destruction introduced by Satan through Adam's failure. Through Abram, God initiated a new family and a new nation, carrying forward His promise to bless all people and undo the corruption Adam had allowed.

This promise came with a severe warning: God would curse anyone who dishonored Abram. This warning about a curse was not new—it was the condition of all people after Adam's failure and expulsion from the garden. Those who rejected God's messages chose to remain under the curse of the fall. Under previous covenants, people accessed God's blessings through faith in His promises and instructions. Today, it is through faith in Christ Jesus that we inherit all of God's promised blessings. The warning not to dishonor Abram was critical because God's promised blessings to redeem the world would come only through Abram's family.

Key Promises to Abraham

- Abraham would father a son in his old age.
- His family would multiply and become as numerous as the stars in the sky.
- His descendants would inherit the land God led him to.

God also foretold:

> *Know for certain that your descendants will be strangers in a country that isn't theirs, and they will be enslaved and oppressed for four hundred years. But I will execute judgment on the nation they serve, and afterward they will come out with great possessions"* (Genesis 15:13–14).

Abram obeyed God's voice and believed His promises, "so he counted him as righteous" (Genesis 15:6). Through Abram's faith and God's providence, his name was changed to Abraham, meaning "Father of a Great Nation." Abraham's promised son, Isaac, carried the covenant forward, as did Isaac's son Jacob. God's promises were passed to each generation, expanding His kingdom and furthering His purpose to reverse the curse from Adam's fall.

Just as Abram's name was changed to Abraham, Jacob's name was changed to Israel. Through Israel's 12 sons, the family grew into the nation of Israel. Over time, Israel became closely identified with God, referring to Him as the God of Abraham, Isaac, and Jacob. This title emphasized that the promises given to each patriarch were passed through the family and nation. Although Israel did not perfectly keep the covenant, the prophetic promises gave them identity, hope, and courage through the centuries. Ultimately, it was the Lord's faithfulness that bonded Abraham, Isaac, and Israel to Him, revealing the enduring power of His promises.

It is significant to note that God desires to give us a name as we obey His promises (Revelation 2:17). In contrast, trying to make a name for ourselves—rooted in pride—is always a mistake, as repeatedly shown in Scripture.

The next major covenant came through Abraham's descendant Moses. Known as the Mosaic Covenant or the Old Covenant, it began with personal promises given to Moses through his encounter with God in Exodus 3:4–12:

> *When the Lord saw he'd gone over to look, God called to him from the midst of the bush, "Moses! Moses!" And he replied, "Here I am." And then he said, "Don't come any closer. Take your sandals off your feet, for the place on which you are standing is holy ground." He also said, "I am the God of your father, the God of Abraham, the God of Isaac, and the God of Jacob." Moses hid his face, because he was afraid to look at God. And the Lord said, "I have surely seen the affliction of my people in Egypt—heard their cries of distress because of their slavemasters' cruelty. I know their sufferings. So I have come down to rescue them from the power of the Egyptians and to bring them up from that land to a good and spacious land, a land flowing with milk and honey—the place of the Canaanites, Hittites, Amorites, Perizzites, Hivites, and Jebusites. For indeed, the cries of the Israelites have reached me, and I've seen how the Egyptians are oppressing them. Come now, for I am sending you to Pharaoh to bring my people, the children of Israel, out of Egypt." But Moses said to God, "Who am I that I should go to Pharaoh and bring the Israelites out of Egypt?" God said, "I will be with you, and this will be the sign to you that it is I who have sent you: When you have brought the people out of Egypt, you will worship God on this mountain."*

The Lord fulfilled His promise, empowering Moses to lead Israel out of Egypt, through the Red Sea, and to the mountain God had chosen.

8 *The God of Your Promises*

There, He continues to give His promises to the people through Moses, as recorded in Exodus 19:1–9:

> *In the third month after the Israelites left Egypt, they moved from Rephidim to the Wilderness of Sinai and encamped in the wilderness before the mountain. Then Moses went up to God, and the* LORD *called to him from the mountain: "Tell the house of Jacob, the people of Israel, 'You saw what I did to Egypt, and how I bore you on wings of eagles and brought you to myself. Now, if you truly heed my voice and keep my covenant* (promises), *you will be my treasured possession out of all the peoples. Though the whole earth is mine to choose from, you shall be to me a kingdom of priests and a holy nation.' These are the words that you are to speak to the Israelites." So, Moses went down and called the elders of the people and set before them all these words* (promises) *the* LORD *had commanded him to speak. And all the people answered together, "We will do all the* LORD *has spoken." So Moses brought their answer back to the* LORD. *The* LORD *told him, "Listen, I am going to come to you in a dense cloud, so the people will hear as I talk with you and will always trust you"* (Emphasis and additions mine).

Moses continued to encounter God, and each time God spoke to him, the Lord faithfully fulfilled His promises and purposes: to reverse the curse and restore the kingdom of God on earth. The Mosaic Covenant, filled with God's promises, was intended to empower the new nation to follow Him and become a light to all other nations, revealing the Living God to humanity. God desired for Israel to be a source of blessing through which He could bless all the peoples of the world.

God Has Always Kept His Promises; People Consistently Break Them

Sadly, after the Lord made this covenant with Israel, the people quickly acted unfaithfully and broke it. The covenant promised blessings of fruitfulness if obeyed and barrenness and brokenness if disobeyed. Yet, the Lord remained faithful to Israel and never broke His covenant. He treated them as His children, but they rejected Him as their God and Creator.

Though Israel spurned His love and discarded His promises, the Lord providentially cared for them. In His love, He remained faithful, disciplining them through the consequences of their own choices while upholding His covenant.

God Promised a King to Fulfill All His Promises

The Lord, ever the promise keeper, gave further assurance of His faithful love through David, the king of Israel. This new agreement, the Davidic Covenant, included the promise that a son of David would one day rule the nations. God would send the Messiah King to restore everything lost through Adam's rejection of God.

This King would uphold all of God's promises, redeem Israel, and bring blessing to all nations. Through Him, the promises made to Noah, Abraham, Isaac, Jacob, Moses, and the nation of Israel—as well as those given by every prophet—would be fulfilled. Despite God's faithful acts and promises, Israel continued to turn away from Him. Yet God never broke His covenant. He sent prophets time and again to remind the leaders and the people of the promises they had made to the Lord through Moses.

God Was Faithful to His Promises

When Israel remembered their covenant commitments and returned to God, He empowered them to repent. When they repented, He renewed His promises, helped them, and restored them. However, when they rebelled, the Lord allowed them to face the consequences He had promised. Through all of Israel's failed faithfulness, God remained steadfast, fulfilling His promises even as their iniquity grew.

Eventually, the nation reached the point where their rebellion could no longer be ignored. God divided the nation into two parts: the northern kingdom, called Israel, and the southern kingdom, known as Judah. The northern tribes were the first to reject the Lord and rebel against Him.

They received His judgment and were ultimately removed from the land of promise.

Years later, the southern kingdom of Judah followed the same path of rebellion. They too faced the consequences of their iniquity and were cast out of the promised land. Yet, in His faithful kindness, God preserved a remnant of Abraham's family, bringing them back to the land so the blessings promised to Abraham, Moses, and David could be fulfilled.

God's great love for humanity is evident in His faithful mercy toward the descendants of Abraham. When they humbled themselves before Him, He blessed them. When they chose to rebel and reject His promises, He allowed them to reap what they had sown. Those who faithfully followed God and His promises were always rewarded, while those who rejected Him and His ways were permitted to face the consequences of their choices. In both cases, God always kept His promises and fulfilled His Word.

In Christ Jesus, God Fulfilled All His Promises

The final covenant, which fulfilled all of God's promises, was established and kept by God's King and David's Son, Christ Jesus. The coming Son of David, Son of Man, and Messiah King was the One:

- Who would crush the serpent's head (Genesis 3:15).
- Through whom all nations would be blessed (Genesis 22:18).
- Born of a virgin (Isaiah 7:14).
- Born in Bethlehem and called Wonderful Counselor, Mighty God, Everlasting Father, and Prince of Peace (Isaiah 9:6; Micah 5:2).
- Who held God's scepter as the Lion of the tribe of Judah (Genesis 49:10; Revelation 5:5).
- Who was the great Prophet to speak God's word (Deuteronomy 18:15–18).
- Referred to as God's Anointed (Psalm 2).
- Who was the Redeemer that would suffer on the cross and save His people (Psalm 22).
- Who was the Suffering Servant, bearing our sins, pierced for our transgressions, and securing our peace with God (Isaiah 53).

- Who was the Holy One who would rise from the grave and never see corruption or decay (Psalm 16:10).
- Who fulfilled over 300 prophesies promised about the coming Messiah King.

When Jesus Christ, Son of David and Son of Man, reveals His mission and purpose, He boldly proclaims, "Repent, because the kingdom of heaven is near" (Matthew 3:2). His coming made all the promises God had ever given to humanity available and accessible. He opened the way into the kingdom of heaven for all who would trust in Him.

Jesus is the Promise Keeper revealed in human form. This covenant was not limited to one person or nation; it was extended to all people of all nations. It is filled with the promises God offered to you when you placed your faith in Jesus Christ.

The New Covenant: God's Promises Made Personal

Jesus Christ, the Messianic King, established the final covenant, fulfilling the prophecies of Jeremiah and Ezekiel under the dispensation of the Mosaic Covenant. The writer of Hebrews explains the purpose of this covenant in Hebrews 8:7–12, revealing why it was necessary:

> *If there had been nothing wrong with the first covenant, no place would have been sought for the second. But when God found fault with the people, he said, "Look! The days are coming, declares the Lord, when I will establish a new covenant with the house of Israel and with the house of Judah. It will not be like the covenant I made with their ancestors at the time when I took them by the hand to lead them out of the land of Egypt because they did not continue living within my covenant, and I turned away from them, declares the Lord. For this is the covenant I will establish with the house of Israel after those days, declares the Lord. I will put my laws in their minds and write them on their hearts. I will be their God, and they will be my people. Each person will no longer teach their neighbor or say to their brother or sister, 'Know*

the Lord,' because they will all know me, from the least of them to the greatest. For I will forgive their wrongdoing and remember their sins no more."

The prophet Ezekiel also spoke of this covenant in Ezekiel 36:16–27, where God, through Ezekiel, expresses His anguish over Israel's failure to keep the Mosaic Covenant and His unwavering commitment to fulfill His promises. In this passage, you can hear God's deep sorrow over Israel's unfaithfulness, yet also His resolute dedication to uphold His holy name and honor by bringing about the new covenant:

The word of the Lord came to me: "Son of man, when the Israelites were living on their land, they defiled it with their ways and their deeds. Their ways were like the uncleanness of menstruation in my presence. So I poured out my wrath on them for all the blood they poured out on the ground, for they defiled it with their idols. I scattered them among the nations and dispersed them among the countries. I judged them according to their ways and deeds. Israel came to the nations, and wherever they went they profaned my holy name, because it was said about them, 'These are the Lord's people, but they were exiled from his land.' Then I was concerned for my holy name when the Israelites profaned it among the nations where they went. Therefore tell the Israelites: 'The Lord God says this: I am not acting for your sakes, O Israelites, but for my holy name, which you have profaned among the nations when you went there. I will prove the holiness of my great name, which has been profaned among the nations, which you profaned among them. Then, when I show myself to be holy among you before their eyes, the nations will know that I am the Lord, declares the Lord God. I will take you from the nations, gather you from all the countries, and bring you into your own land. I'll sprinkle clean water on you, and you'll be clean. I'll cleanse you from all your uncleanness and idols, and I will give you a new heart—put a new spirit within you, remove your heart of stone from your bodies, and* *give you a heart of flesh. I will put my Spirit within you and cause you to follow my statutes and to be careful to follow my ordinances.'"*

This should be both comforting and empowering as you reflect on how deeply committed Father God is to the promises and messages He has given you.

Jesus Christ, God Incarnate, Is the Promise Keeper Who Honors the Lord's Holy Name

Jesus Christ instituted this final covenant at the Last Supper, calling it the "new covenant." Luke 22:20 records the moment, "He took the cup, saying, 'This cup, is the new covenant in my blood, which is poured out for you.'" It is important to understand that the "you," in this verse refers to the disciples who were with Him at the Last Supper, before He went to the cross. These disciples were Jews and symbolized the "house of Israel" and "the house of Judah" (Hebrews 8:8), the original recipients of Jeremiah's prophesy in Jeremiah 31:31–34. Jesus clarifies in Matthew 15:24 that He "was sent only to the lost sheep of Israel." However, the promise to Abraham declared that through him, "all the peoples on earth will be blessed" (Genesis 12:3). This universal blessing to all believers is affirmed by the apostle Paul in Romans 1:16, "I am not ashamed of the gospel because it is the instrument of God's power that brings salvation for everyone who believes—to the Jews first and also to the Gentile." Through Christ, the new covenant extends to all who believe, fulfilling God's promises to both Israel and the nations.

This Is the Covenant God Made with You through Jesus Christ

This new covenant was made with you personally to establish a direct and intimate relationship between you and God. In this covenant, God is the keeper of the promises He has made to you. You are as important to Him as Abraham, Moses, David, Peter, Paul, or any other hero of the Bible. This truth is why Peter writes in 2 Peter 1:1, "To those who have received a faith of the same kind as ours." This covenant is a unilateral agreement in which God made all the promises and took full responsibility for keeping them, by working through Jesus Christ.

The God-man, Jesus Christ, retraced Adam's missteps on behalf of all humanity. Through Christ, God redeemed everything Adam lost. Jesus bore the penalty for sin by taking the sins of the entire world upon Himself, thereby crushing the head and authority of the serpent. In that spiritual battle, however, Satan inflicted the metaphoric bruise on the Lord's heel as Jesus gave His life for the world.

This covenant, along with all its promises, was initiated on the last night Jesus spent with His disciples and culminated His work on the earth. That is why, as he hung on the cross, He proclaims, "It is finished" (John 19:30). Everything God required, and all that humanity needed to be restored to complete harmony with Him, was accomplished through Jesus Christ.

This was the ultimate reason the second person of the Godhead came to earth as the incarnate Son of God: to fulfill all the promises and prophesies God had given to humanity. Jesus Christ, born of the Virgin Mary and crucified by the Romans, revealed the Living God through His miracles, teachings, and actions. Ultimately, His death, burial, and resurrection were the greatest demonstration of God's promise-keeping power.

Through His sacrificial death, Jesus poured out of His blood for the forgiveness of sins. As Paul writes, "God made Jesus, the one who had no sin, to be the sin offering for us so that in him we might become the righteousness of God" (2 Corinthians 5:21). His resurrection from the dead proved that the serpent's head had been crushed and that Satan's authority, gained through Adam's rebellion, was broken for all who choose to believe in God's promises through Christ Jesus. Through Jesus' death, burial, and resurrection, the reversal of the curse began to manifest in this world.

That is why the apostle Paul confidently declares, "All the promises of God are 'Yes' (i.e., *fulfilled*) in [Jesus Christ]. Therefore through him we speak 'Amen' (i.e., *so be it*) to the glory of God" (2 Corinthians 1:20).

The God Revealed in Christ Jesus Is the Promise Keeper

The God of your promises—the One who has spoken His Word as promises, laws, testimonies, statutes, principles, commands, instructions, judgments, precepts, regulations, and rules—is a faithful God and the ultimate keeper of His Word. He is able to fulfill all He has spoken to you if you will say "Amen" through faithful obedience, partaking of Christ's divine nature.

As you reflect on what it means to fully embrace the new covenant and allow God to fulfill His promises through you, consider these faith-building truths from the chapter you just read:

1. God has fulfilled and continues to fulfill every promise through Jesus Christ. Remember, "Jesus Christ is the same yesterday and today and forever" (Hebrews 13:8). The same faith you have is the faith Peter had because you believe in the same God: Jesus Christ!
2. None of the Bible's heroes, Old Testament or New Testament, could have imagined how God would use their faithful obedience to bring the kingdom of heaven to earth.
3. Those who encountered God's glory and goodness, and received His great and precious promises, could not fully conceive of how God would fulfill them.

Adam could not have foreseen how one of his "descendants" (Genesis 12:7) would crush the serpent's head. Yet God fulfilled that promise through Jesus Christ on the cross. Abraham was overwhelmed when God promised he would be the father of a great nation, with descendants as numerous as the stars. By faith, Abraham believed God, and his faith was credited as righteousness. In the same way, God will honor your faith as you trust in Him.

It wasn't just the well-known heroes of faith who participated in God's promises. Consider the unnamed Hebrew midwives who defied Pharaoh and saved Hebrew boys from death in the Nile. Because of their obedience, Moses' life was preserved, and God's kingdom promises advanced.

Take King David as another example. He believed, yet likely never fully understood, that his descendant would be God's Son. The promised

King from David's line would not only rule over Israel but over the entire universe.

Choose any faithful person from the Bible, and you will find that even though they were imperfect, God carried His promises forward, fulfilling them far beyond what they could have asked or imagined. Embrace the wisdom and catch the vision that you will not fully comprehend the magnificent and great precious promises you've been given until you reach heaven's shore. Nor will you see the full impact of your obedience and faithfulness in daily partaking of the divine nature. That ultimate fulfillment will come when your faith is made complete—when you meet Jesus Christ face to face.

PREFACE TO CHAPTERS 9 AND 10

Pride goes before destruction, and an arrogant spirit goes before stumbling.
PROVERBS 16:18

Weeping may last for a night, but joy comes with the morning.
PSALM 30:5

Before we explore chapters 9 and 10, I want to share more about my journey. While I am now much more fruitful in my relationship with Christ, this has not always been the case. My spiritual growth has been a process, and I believe sharing this will provide valuable context as we move forward.

Chapter 9 will highlight the critical importance of developing consistent spiritual disciplines. The growth you are experiencing in Christ is a result of these disciplines, which enable you to partake of the divine nature. The Holy Spirit uses them to disciple and transform you. My hope is that after reading chapter 9, you will recognize these disciplines as *sacred spaces* where you connect with God. This chapter will also provide guidance on how to deepen and develop additional disciplines and sacred spaces, allowing you to cooperate more intentionally with the Holy Spirit.

Your Relationship with God Is Unique and Precious

One of the pitfalls of learning about spiritual disciplines is the temptation to imitate others who seem to achieve amazing results. When you replicate their practices, you may not experience the same transformation, which leads to frustration. The truth is, you cannot use spiritual disciplines at your whim or will, just as you cannot claim any biblical promise and expect it to produce identical results in your life as it did in someone else's.

Preface to 9 & 10

Every step of our spiritual formation requires humility, like that of a child holding their father's hand. Remember, imitation is futile in the realm of spiritual growth; personal authenticity is the key.

In chapter 10, I will explore what optimizing your relationship with Christ looks like through the metaphors the Bible uses to describe a fruitful life. The Bible reveals this as your inheritance in God—a life that He desires to form in you and through you for His good pleasure.

Before introducing the incredible promises of God that encourage you to look forward in faith, I want to pause to set you up for success. It's easy to read this book up to this point and develop a false expectation about how quickly this process will unfold in your life. Another reason I include this section is to caution you against the misconception that spiritual maturity means you take back control of your soul to live life on your terms. To prevent this, I want to share more about my own journey of growing in faith and how it has shaped my understanding of the spiritual disciplines and the transformative work of the Holy Spirit.

Let's continue this journey together, keeping in mind that God's timing and process for each of us are unique and always rooted in His perfect wisdom and love.

From Failure to Grace

As I wrote in the introduction, I received Christ in 1970 at the age of 19. A few years later, in 1973–74, I began meditating on Psalm 139. This practice was introduced to me through a teacher named Bill Gothard, who led a weeklong event called the *Institute in Basic Youth Conflicts*. During one session, he spoke about God's intricate design for each person, emphasizing the truth found in Psalm 139:16, "Thine eyes did see my substance, yet being unperfect; and in thy book all my members were written, which in continuance were fashioned, when as yet there was none of them" (KJV).

The message I received from this verse was profoundly personal: God had formed me in my mother's womb and, in his wisdom, had planned out my life. That night, surrounded by thousands of people in an auditorium, I wept as the Holy Spirit revealed Christ's glorious love for me. Through His glory, goodness, and grace, I received the promise that God had a purpose and plan for my life.

At that moment, I could not have imagined how that verse would change my life. I already knew God had chosen me—John 15:16 was a personal promise to me—but I struggled with a poor self-image and lack of confidence. Psalm 139:16 gave me hope, a promise that God's plan for me was infused with His transformative love.

The next evening, the session was about meditating on Scripture. I immediately decided to meditate on Psalm 139:16. After the conference, I began to memorize the entire psalm, meditating on it daily and exploring related Scriptures.

My commitment deepened into a discipline. I rose early to read, study, pray, and contemplate Psalm 139. This intensive seeking went on for weeks until one morning, as I knelt in prayer, I experienced an overwhelming sense of God's love for me. I wept deeply as years of emotional pain and loneliness poured out, replaced by the love and the presence of Christ in a way I had never known before.

At that time, I was serving as an assistant pastor. On Sunday mornings, I sat on stage with the other pastoral leaders during worship. That week, as we sang, the joy of Christ's love and peace radiated through me. I became completely lost in the presence of the Lord.

After the service, several people approached me independently, asking what had happened—they could see something different about me. I was surprised but shared what I had experienced earlier that week as I prayed through Psalm 139. I knew whatever the Spirit had done within me was the result of seeking Christ through His promises. That moment marked a profound change in my life—one rooted in the hope and truth of God's Word.

Knowledge Puffs Up; Love Builds Up

Despite my transformative encounter with God, I was still very immature. I did not yet understand the revelation Peter teaches in the first chapter of his second letter, the foundation of this book. I didn't grasp that God was just beginning to transform my mind and conform my life to allow Christ Jesus to live through me. I didn't realize I had been given a magnificent promise that was my path to continually partake of the divine nature. Looking back, I now understand that I did partake of the divine nature during that powerful encounter with the Holy Spirit. I didn't know that this was meant to be an ongoing *pathway to live* a strong, vibrant life for God. While some of my deep wounds were healed, I didn't fully comprehend how much more work God needed to do in my heart.

Pride Goes before a Fall

Encountering God when you are brokenhearted and hurting is not uncommon. Neither is what happened to me afterward. Because I didn't understand 2 Peter 1, I assumed God had blessed me and that it was now up to me to live my life the best way I could to please Him. I fell into the same trap as Adam's sin, thinking I knew what was good and evil and that I could determine the *best way to live for God*. That attitude, of course, is called pride.

Over time, I drifted away from daily meditation. I remained in my church position, still leading others, reading my Bible, and praying. I was even more persuasive and confident in sharing Christ because of my transformative encounter with God, and I spoke about it with boldness and conviction. But I wasn't as intentional or earnest in seeking God as I had been. The pressures of life—work, marriage, and college (yes, I was still enrolled)—crowded out my zeal to seek the Lord. Feeling more self-confident, I leaned into my religious path as a young pastor. Sadly, I didn't realize how much I was slipping back into my own ways. As Scripture teaches, a branch not abiding in the vine will wither. Slowly, I began to wither. Yet, Father God wasn't finished with me and didn't allow me to drift completely away from Him.

I continued to study and teach Psalm 139, but I never again experienced the same intimate encounter with the presence of God as I had that morning decades earlier. I would return to the passage to instruct others and grow in my biblical knowledge, but I wasn't humbly and consistently partaking of the divine nature as 2 Peter 1:3–4 teaches.

In 1981, I started my first church, which grew rapidly with weekly attendance averaging 300–400 people. God was faithful, but I began to drift into unholy behaviors. My pride grew alongside my public ministry. I became more arrogant and demanding of my wife, my family, and others. In 1990, this destructive pride culminated in my decision to leave the church I had started. Two years later, my first marriage ended in a heartbreaking divorce.

This was a very dark time for my family and me. I was broken in every sense. Yet God, in His grace, remained faithful. I knew He loved me and wouldn't leave me, but He also wouldn't tolerate my destructive pride and behavior. Through repentance and deep humility, I began rebuilding my relationship with God and others. I became intentional again about seeking Him through His promises.

During this season, God opened an unexpected door for ministry. I began serving at a small wedding chapel, officiating marriages. Over three years, I married hundreds of couples and counseled each one on how to stay married! God, in His wisdom, used this time to discipline and restore me. It was during this period that I met Eunice, my present wife. By God's grace, we have been married for more than 32 years. Today, we are more in love than when we first began, a testimony to God's redemptive power and unfailing grace.

Humility Is Key to Discipleship

My point in sharing the dark side of my story is to prevent you from having a false picture of my spiritual journey. In the preceding chapters, I may have painted a picture that Peter gave us a fast and effortless way to become optimal in our relationship with Christ.

I am sure you know that Jesus said that following Him would involve a cross. In Jesus' day, crosses were carried only by people walking towards death. All who truly follow Him must understand and learn that unless you are willing to die to your own way, you will never become the fruitful image bearer of Christ. I am still learning and growing in the knowledge and grace of God, and you will too if you choose to continue to follow Him.

I did recover from my years of rebellion. However, recovery is different from becoming an optimal disciple. God patiently and continually encouraged me with many promises like, "He who began a good work in you will bring it to completion until the day of Christ Jesus" (Philippians 1:6).

Incidentally, in the 1990s, this verse from Philippians was often sung as a praise chorus. It was the song I chose as the final song at the last service I led in the first church I started—before the people who loved me discovered the depth of my immaturity and hypocrisy, and before my life unraveled. I genuinely wanted them to continue trusting God, despite my failings, and to remain steadfast in their faith.

I am thankful that God preserved many of them. In time, He sent a worthy pastor who built a thriving church from the ruins I left behind. That church, now under a different name, remains a strong witness for Christ in San Antonio.

> *The way of the righteous is like the dawning light that shines brighter and brighter until full daylight.*
> **Proverbs 4:18**

In 1997, after seven years of recovery, rebuilding, and restoring my soul and relationship with my children, the Lord opened the door for me to establish a second church in San Antonio called Redeemer's Hope. This congregation remained a small church, with Sunday attendance hovering around 60–70 people for most of the 17 years I led it, never growing beyond 100 attendees. As a bi-vocational pastor, I worked seven days a week, balancing my role as a public school teacher and my responsibilities as the church's leader.

Yet, I still lacked a clear understanding of how spiritual formation truly happens or how to disciple others effectively. While I knew how to lead people to Christ and help them begin their walk with Him, and I was teaching the Bible and preaching solid sermons about God's nature and His love for us, I didn't fully grasp how to help people consistently partake of the divine nature through their personal promises from God. This is the core teaching of 2 Peter 1, and at the time, it was a significant gap in my understanding of discipleship.

God's Ways Are Not Our Ways

Looking back, I now see that Christ was faithful to continue discipling me, even though I was not consistently in an optimal relationship with Him. While I had repented and was growing into a healthy and holy life with my wife and others, I still didn't fully grasp the critical importance of continually seeking God humbly through His promises.

A major turning point came in 2009 when I and the church leaders were faced with the deceptive life of our youth pastor/praise leader. He was leading a double life that ultimately destroyed his marriage—a story painfully familiar to me. When confronted by the elders and me, he chose to leave the fellowship and divorce his wife.

I felt an overwhelming sense of failure—not just for him and his wife, but for the church I pastored. I had been doing everything I knew to do, yet it was clearly not enough. In my grief and desire to heal our wounded congregation, I sought a deeper understanding of marriage and how to strengthen the marriages in our church.

I had a library full of books that focused on making marriage "happy," with advice centered on pleasing your spouse to get your own needs met. Unfortunately, starting with self-focus in any relationship is a recipe for failure. Thankfully, during a trip to a local Bible bookstore, I came across a book whose subtitle immediately grabbed my attention. Gary Thomas' *Sacred Marriage*. The subtitle asked a challenging question: "What if God designed marriage to make us holy more than to make us happy?"

That question hit me like a much-needed wake-up call. I took the book home and devoured it. As I clung to every word, my understanding of spiritual formation began to transform. Gary Thomas' transparency and depth opened my eyes to my own selfishness. By God's grace, I entered a deeper repentance than I had ever known. At the time, I didn't realize that Christ was using this book to lay the foundation—not only for me to become the husband I desired to be but also to begin uncovering Peter's path to spiritual formation.

Struggling to Find Consistency

Even with these breakthroughs, my relationship with Christ was not consistently optimal. While I was growing, I still struggled to sustain my spiritual zeal. My spiritual life resembled the Israelites in the book of Judges rather than the victories described in the book of Joshua. I cycled between spiritual highs and lows, trying one clever idea after another to stay focused on Christ and to build up the people I pastored.

In this frustration, the Lord led me to start a monthly men's breakfast focused on one key question: How do you make a disciple? Over time, I began asking the men in the group: How is Christ discipling you? What moves the needle in your spiritual life? Although we never reached a clear answer, I knew we were asking the right questions.

Teaching without a Clear Blueprint

During the 17 years of pastoring my second church, my approach to spiritual formation followed the traditional focus of many churches: encouraging people to read the Bible, pray, give, witness to their faith, and serve. I passionately taught about the importance of having a personal relationship with God, as Scripture teaches. Yet I found it difficult to explain and transfer to them how to truly develop that relationship.

I had experienced God's presence when I was radically saved and knew that He had been with me through the darkest moments of my sin. I also knew I could connect with God when meditating on favorite passages like Psalm 139 and John 15:1–17. But I didn't fully understand how important it was to **consistently** partake of the divine nature through my personalized promises as Peter outlines in 2 Peter 1.

So I taught people what I knew. I shared ideas that had helped me. I read and preached persuasive sermons urging them to live a godly, morally upright life. But I couldn't shake the feeling that I was just giving people a new set of moral rules to follow each week.

Make no mistake—I believed in grace. I knew my recovery and restoration were entirely by God's grace. Yet I still wasn't living in the fullness of Christ's way. I thought I was, and when I compared myself to others, I felt I was doing well. But deep inside, I still had unanswered questions about how to make a disciple and how to follow Christ consistently and closely.

Now hear this: Everyone who is thirsty, come to the water!
Isaiah 55:1

A Breakthrough in My Journey

A breakthrough came in late 2010 when I sensed the Lord calling me to spend more time meditating on Scripture. I committed to rising an hour earlier each morning to seek Him in prayer and through His Word. During that season, the Lord led me to memorize and meditate on Isaiah 55. It became a transformative time, and I regained much of the joy and zeal I had experienced when I first came to Christ. The truths in Isaiah 55 were so rich and life-giving that I dedicated my last two years of preaching and teaching at Redeemer's Hope Church to this passage. In the final year, I challenged the congregation to join my wife, Eunice, and me in memorizing it. While some memorized parts of it, most did not engage with it as I had hoped. I was disappointed, certain that this passage was a wellspring of living water essential for a fruitful spiritual life.

What I didn't understand at the time was that Isaiah 55 was *my* path—God's specific personalized seed promise to empower me to partake of His divine nature—but it wasn't necessarily meant for everyone. Years later, I realized that while Isaiah 55 was a powerful and transformative promise for me, I couldn't impose it on others. In my zeal to share the life-giving truth I had rediscovered, I wanted everyone to experience it as I had, just as Psalm 139 and John 15:16 had impacted me decades earlier. Of course, this approach didn't work. I now see that meditating on Isaiah 55 was part of *my* personal promises and discipline. It was a genuine experience of partaking in the divine nature, but I couldn't make it someone else's path. This failure taught me the absolute importance of the individualized process Peter outlines in 2 Peter 1.

Discovering Your Personal Promises

As I've emphasized in this book, God must open your eyes to see the seed promises He has personally given you. Each person, with the help of the Holy Spirit, must discern their own unique path and the personalized promises God uses to disciple them into partaking of Christ's divine nature.

Your first love for Jesus Christ is the beginning of this personal relationship with Him, but moralistic religion or rigid rules of righteousness cannot sustain that love. The only way Isaiah 55—or any passage—will transform you as it has transformed me is if the Holy Spirit reveals it to you as a personal promise and you commit to cultivating it with loving discipline. When led by the Spirit, this process transforms your mind, renews your spirit, and gives you the grace to think His thoughts and live His ways. That is exactly what 2 Peter 1 teaches!

Redeemer's Hope Church closed its doors after 17 years because I felt I had shared everything I knew about Christ and spiritual growth. In 2014, I stepped down as lead pastor. Eunice and I began attending another church, assisting the pastor in any way we could. Many people from Redeemer's Hope joined us at the new church, though most eventually found other congregations. We stayed at that church for five years, blessed by the ministry of a godly pastor. In 2019, the Holy Spirit led us to move to the beautiful mountains of Tennessee, where we embarked on a new chapter in our journey.

I Hadn't Yet Discovered How Christ Was Disciplining Me

Providentially, between 2010 and 2020, I began a consistent pattern of meditating on the special passages I had received since I first believed. During this time, I became increasingly aware of God's grace and favor in my life. However, I still didn't fully understand the pattern and process outlined in 2 Peter 1. While I was walking on the path of cooperating with Christ's discipleship in my life, I lacked clarity on how to encourage others to consistently walk in the Spirit with Christ. Without Peter's blueprint, I led others based on how I believed God was leading me, which was my own way, but not theirs.

This is no small issue because unless we understand God's ways, we will, with the best intentions, lead people in our ways instead of His. We may know how God has worked in us, but love is what we need to build others up. Peter's path, in 2 Peter 1 is one of loving God at every step. It requires us to walk humbly with Him so that He can love others through us in His way. I urge you to call out, in deep humility, for God to teach you His way and for Christ to reveal how Peter's path aligns with your personal journey. Understanding this will empower you to become the optimal disciple you long to be and equip you to disciple others in harmony with God's Spirit.

Even after God led us to Erwin, Tennessee, I found myself asking the same questions: How do I know I am living optimally in my relationship with Christ? How do I make a disciple? Finally, God providentially directed my steps toward the insights I now share in this book. Through prayerful study of 2 Peter 1, I sensed the Holy Spirit guiding me to these truths in a way that profoundly shaped my understanding. I must emphasize: I did not receive this message about 2 Peter 1 from any other person or author.

The Light Came On

God revealed that His glory and goodness were the keys to understand the promises He uniquely gives to each of us. I realized that every time I had received a transformative message, it was because the light of His glory had shone in my heart, revealing some aspect of His wondrous and beautiful nature. Through these encounters with Christ's glory and goodness, I was given the precious promises that enabled me to participate in the divine nature and be transformed into His image.

Eureka! I finally understood! I now know what I need to do and how to disciple others by helping them explore their personal story and relationship with Christ through Spirit-led questions.

Your Unique Connection with God

It is vital to understand and embrace the personal and unique way God connects with you through the promises and messages He gives you. Diligently, humbly, and intentionally wait on the Lord to open your spiritual eyes to how He has been discipling you.

I am now confident, not in myself, but in God and His Word, as I walk the optimal discipleship path of seeking Him daily. My focus remains on the precious promises He has given me, starting from my earliest days of trusting Christ. The Holy Spirit continues to add new promises as I need them, each one transformative, full of grace and truth, and brimming with eternal life.

Preface to 9 & 10

God's Word as My Foundation

Psalm 139 has been a comforting revelation of my identity in Christ. His adoptive love, has been a constant reassurance, guiding me even in my darkest valleys and willful sinfulness. Even when I found myself in the depths of despair, His hand led me, and His right hand held me.

John 15:1–17 infused His love and confidence in me, revealing the transformative power of abiding in Christ and His Word. This knowledge filled me with hope and confidence in God's desire to answer my prayers and produce fruitfulness through the True Vine.

Isaiah 55 has become a pathway for me to experience spiritual power. It has strengthened my faith and confidence in the ability of God's Word to fulfill all that His Spirit speaks into my soul.

Psalm 51 deepened my repentance and humility, though I know I will never fully attain the fullness of God's plan on this side of eternity.

The Path to Optimal Discipleship

Since intentionally meditating on 2 Peter 1, I've come to see it as the clear path to spiritual maturity—a way to become more fruitful and effective in knowing Christ. This is the blueprint for becoming an optimal disciple of Jesus Christ.

God desires to do far more in you and through you than you could ask or imagine. Hearing my story in its fullness should offer you grace—for yourself and for those you disciple.

I pray that as you read chapter 9, you will be inspired and convicted to commit to developing sacred spaces where God can fill you with the wind of His Spirit. May He open your eyes to the organic metaphors in Scripture that reveal your unlimited potential when you follow Peter's plan. Father God desires you to become fruitful and effective in knowing Christ Jesus so that you may reverse the curse in your world and end your earthly journey with a grand entrance into heaven!

CHAPTER 9

Cultivating His Magnificent Promises

If anyone desires to do his will, they will know whether the teaching is from God or whether I speak from myself.
JOHN 7:17

At this point in your study, as you seek to become optimal in your walk with Christ, you should have discerned one or more of God's great and precious promises specifically given to you. These personalized promises are messages of hope, love, peace, healing, spiritual vision, and more. You likely have some understanding of why these hold such deep significance to you.

Your next step is both practical and personal: discerning how the Holy Spirit has led you into disciplines of humility that will engraft the Word into your mind, heart, and soul. This involves applying your heart to understanding the attitudes and processes that will allow the Word to take root deeply within you. The Word of God is meant to be implanted or grafted into your soul, growing into a fruitful tree of life that fulfills His eternal purpose for you.

You may have noticed a tendency to be more like the person described in James' epistle—one who only hears the Word but does not act on it. James' description reveals the nature of a shallow spiritual life. If you desire to become optimal in your relationship with God, you must become a doer of His Word—a person who continually abides in Christ and His Word:

> *Be doers of God's Word and not just hearers, who deceive themselves. For anyone who is a hearer of the word and not a doer is like a person who examines their natural face in a mirror, and after looking, goes away and immediately forgets what kind of person they are. But the person who looks intently at the perfect law, that of freedom, and continues in it (who is not a forgetful hearer but has become a doer of the work), will be blessed in their work* (James 1:22–25).

Our destiny will not be fulfilled by simply hearing or receiving God's promise. You must become a "doer," but not through your own strength, wisdom, or power. To glorify your Father in heaven and bear fruit, you must engraft His promised message into your life. Like the good soil in the Parable of the Sower, God intends for you to be productive and effective in understanding your knowledge of Him. Jesus made it clear in John 7:17 that if we want to know His Word is truth, we must put it into practice. Yet the only way we can do this for His glory is by His grace! He longs for us to glorify Him so that He can make a name for us, rather than us striving to make a name for ourselves.

A Space for Cultivating Divine Life

To be productive and fruitful, His power and life must grow in you and through you. This requires a space in your soul under constant cultivation. Imagine this sacred space as a beautiful garden where you cooperate with Father God to become a spiritual gardener. Just as God placed Adam and Eve in a garden, we are also designed to be nourished and find beauty in our spiritual growth.

Gardens are places of continual nourishment, and when humankind has a steady supply of nutritional food, they flourish. Spiritually, we need to constantly "taste and see that the LORD is good" to take refuge in him (Psalm 34:8). This is how God has always sustained the faith of his people through the deserts and wildernesses of life.

It is no surprise that the often-quoted words "people shall not live on bread alone" (Matthew 4:4) were first spoken by God to people struggling to live in the wilderness. Moses records these thoughts from the mouth of God, emphasizing the role of His Word in sustaining faith:

> *Remember how he humbled you; how he let you hunger and fed you with manna, which neither you, nor your ancestors knew of, that he might make known to you that people do not live by bread alone. Rather, they live by every word that comes from the mouth of the* L<small>ORD</small> (Deuteronomy 8:3).

Only as you live in the light of the promises God has given you and feast on His truth will you know God as He is. Through that reflection, you will see both yourself and Him accurately, enabling you to yield to His grace and be used for His glory.

Humbly Accept the Word Planted in You

James 1:21 says, "Humbly receive the word implanted in you, which can save your souls." James reveals the essential attitude for implanting God's promises in your heart by emphasizing humility. Your humble cooperation with the Holy Spirit is the key to continual spiritual growth. God resists the proud but gives grace to the humble to accomplish His will. He desires you to become "impregnated" with truth so that you can manifest His life in the world, revealing His character.

Your humility before God and faith in His promises, revealed to you through the glory of Christ, are the means by which you walk in step with the Holy Spirit. Consider the conception of Jesus Christ by the Virgin Mary. While her story in Luke's Gospel of conceiving God's Son is historically true and unique, it also serves as a symbolic lesson for your spiritual journey. Just as Mary brought the Son of God into the world in the flesh, we are called to bring forth the kingdom of God into the world through our lives. To manifest the kingdom in this world, King Jesus must live in you and through you.

You've likely heard the Christmas story countless times and perhaps even watched children reenact the angel's visit to Mary with delight. Yet Mary's story holds significant insights into your spiritual journey. In this

9 Cultivating His Magnificent Promises

process, the Holy Spirit opens your spiritual ears to hear and your spiritual eyes to see His ways:

> *In the sixth month of Elizabeth's pregnancy, God sent the angel Gabriel to a town in Galilee called Nazareth, to a virgin betrothed to a man named Joseph, a descendant of David. The virgin's name was Mary. The angel went to her and said, "Greetings, favored one. The Lord is with you. [Blessed are you among women.]" When Mary heard this, she was perplexed and wondered what it meant. The angel continued, "Do not be afraid, Mary, for you have found favor with God. And listen, now you will conceive in your womb and give birth to a son, and you are to name him Jesus. He will be great and will be called the Son of the Most High. The Lord God will give him the throne of his ancestral father David, and he will reign over the house of Jacob forever, for his kingdom will never end"* (Luke 1:26–38).

Mary experiences God's glory and goodness through her encounter with the angel Gabriel. His greeting, "Greetings, favored one. The Lord is with you. [Blessed are you among women]" was not how she perceived herself. Similarly, you must receive God's identity for you to embrace and conceive His promises.

In Mary's case, the angel's evaluation of her was overwhelmingly positive, and she faithfully believed it. Yet, keep in mind that God often meets us in our weakest moments. He uses our sin, guilt, shame, and fears to reveal His love, forgiveness, and grace. Experiencing His glorious love enables you to desire and embrace your new identity in Christ. Mary's reaction is typical of anyone who encounters an angel and hears God's view of them—she is troubled, anxious, and fearful:

> *Mary asked the angel, "How can this happen, since I am a virgin?" The angel answered, "The Holy Spirit will come upon you, and the power of the Most High will overshadow you. So the holy one to be born will be called the Son of God. And listen to this: Your relative Elizabeth has conceived*

a son in her old age. She who was said to be barren is in her sixth month. For nothing will be impossible with God!" Mary replied, *"Look, I am the servant of the Lord. May it be done to me as you have said." Then, the angel left her* (Luke 1:34–38).

Your spiritual journey began with an intervention from God. Often, He uses your need to help you realize your dependence on Him and deepen your trust in His Word. However, in Mary's case, the account of the angel's appearance does not mention any specific concerns she was facing. There is no reference to fear, weakness, or worry—she was simply going about her life, preparing to marry Joseph. What this story reveals is that God could break into your life with His glory and presence to impart special promises that expand His kingdom on earth.

The way God brings His kingdom into your world is through your trust in His promises. These promises are the special messages that come to you when you encounter God's glory and goodness. Remember, Jesus taught His followers to pray in the Lord's Prayer, "May your kingdom come, and may your will be done" (Matthew 6:10). This not merely a prayer for Christ's return but a call to experience the present kingdom of heaven being manifested in your present circumstances.

Colossians 1:13–14 reminds us that the Father has "rescued us from the domain of darkness and who has transferred us into the kingdom of his beloved Son, in whom we have redemption [through his blood], the forgiveness of sins." If you trust Christ Jesus as your Savior, you are already part of the kingdom of God. However, only by faith in His promises can you partake of the divine nature (the Holy Spirit's power) to manifest His eternal life in this world.

Mary's Faith Changed the World

When Gabriel tells Mary, "Do not be afraid, Mary, for you have found favor with God," he gave her an overwhelming and humanly impossible task: "Listen, now you will conceive in your womb and give birth to a son, and you are to name him Jesus. He will be great and will be called the Son of the Most High. The Lord God will give him the throne of his

9 Cultivating His Magnificent Promises

ancestral father David, and he will reign over the house of Jacob forever, for his Kingdom, will never end."

Mary was stunned! Her first thought was, *How can I do this?* Focusing on the idea of giving birth to a son, and honoring her virtue and commitment to Joseph, she asks, "How can this happen, since I am a virgin?"

When God reveals the glory and excellence of Christ to your soul, it may address a need in your life, an essential purpose for His kingdom, or both! In Mary's case, it wasn't a need or weakness that prompted God's intervention but His eternal purpose to bring Christ into the world.

Every promise God gives is meant to further His will and ways in your life and reveal Jesus to others. Through your faith in His promises and your faithfulness to them, you become a vessel for building the kingdom of God on earth. Doing God's will is an impossible task without His power working in and through you, but with God, everything He desires to accomplish through you is possible. Often, when God gives a promise, you have no way of knowing the far-reaching impact it will have on others—or even your own life.

Your Promises Are Great and Magnificent!

No "human mind has imagined these are what God has prepared for those who love him" (1 Corinthians 2:9). In the same way, when God gave you His precious promises, you could not have imagined how He would use them to transform your life and impact others. The only way to fully grasp what God has for you in His promises is for them to be "revealed . . . to us by the Holy Spirit" (1 Corinthians 2:10). Your role is to receive God's promises with humility and respond in obedience, as Mary did.

After Mary believed the angel's promise, she visited Elizabeth. When Elizabeth confirmed the promise, Mary responded with joy, breaking into song. As other events in Jesus' life strengthened her faith, Mary "treasured these things and considered them carefully in her heart" (Luke 2:19). Mary's response reveals a key attitude in manifesting God's kingdom: recognizing that His promises and actions are precious, meaningful, and central to your love relationship with Him. Treasure your promises—they are God's messages to guide your life!

Mary's story is well known. She faithfully believed and received, becoming the vessel of God's grace. She gave birth to Jesus, the Son of God, who brought the kingdom of God to earth.

Your Soul as God's Garden of Grace

Your innermost being is like a sacred womb, a hidden place where God creates life. It is designed to be a garden of grace where God plants His promises to produce the fruit of the Spirit, manifesting His kingdom through you. His promises take root in your soul, producing His nature in you.

Through the indwelling message of Christ, faith is birthed, and eternal life is received. This allows God's power to transform you and conform you into the image of His Son. Becoming Christlike is impossible without humble dependence on God's Word and power. Treasure His promises—they are His seeds of grace, meant to grow and flourish in your life.

His Promises Are Seeds; Your Heart Is the Soil

(Note: Review chapters 4 and 5 before continuing, as they lay the foundation for internalizing and living by God's promises—a key aspect of spiritual growth.)

Cultivating God's promises is much like growing a natural seed. It begins with good, soft soil—a heart that is humble and surrendered to God. It also requires the transformative power of God's presence and the life-giving water of the Holy Spirit.

The process must be intentional, consistent, and deeply personal. It is not a method to manipulate God for your desires but a humble and dependent journey in which God reveals Himself to you and through you, empowering and encouraging you along the way.

Understanding the Cultivation Process

The cultivation process is revealed in the Old Testament through the concept of *meditation*. Joshua 1:8 instructs us, "This book of the Law must never depart from your mouth. Meditate on it day and night so that you may be careful to observe all that is written in it, for then you will prosper in your ways. Then you will succeed." Similarly, Psalm 1:2 describes the blessed person as one "whose delight is in the law of the LORD, and who meditates on his law day and night."

Meditate = Abide

In the New Testament, the word *abide* carries a similar meaning. John 15:1–17 strongly emphasizes the absolute necessity of abiding in Christ, the True Vine, to produce spiritual fruit. Verses 4–5 make it clear that without abiding, you will remain fruitless:

> *Abide in me, and I in you. As the branch cannot bear fruit by itself, unless it abides in the vine, neither can you, unless you abide in me. I am the vine; you are the branches. Whoever abides in me and I in him, he it is that bears much fruit, for apart from me, you can do nothing* (ESV).

The connection between the words *meditate* and *abide* is evident in what happens to a person's spiritual life when they cease to do either. Consider John 15:6 and Psalm 1:3. In John 15:6, Jesus says, "If anyone does not abide in me, he is thrown away like a branch and **withers**; and the branches are gathered, thrown into the fire, and burned" (ESV). In contrast, Psalm 1:3 describes the blessed person who meditates on God's Word: "He is like a tree planted by streams of water that yields its fruit in season and whose leaf does not **wither**. Whatever that person does prospers."

In both the Old and New Testaments, the condition of a thriving, prospering soul depends on continual communion with the living God. Whether it's called *abiding in Christ* or *meditating on the Word*, the result is the same: the spiritual life does not wither or grow frail but instead becomes fruitful and prospers.

As 2 Peter 1:8 explains, "For if these qualities *(of godliness that comes from continual partaking of the divine nature)* are in you and increasing, they will keep you from being ineffective or unproductive in the knowledge *(knowing)* of our Lord Jesus Christ" (additions mine). Therefore, the practice of continual abiding and meditative communion with Jesus Christ through His promises is not only essential but also brings joy, fulfillment, and hope to your relationship with God. It becomes a source of strength and guidance, empowering you to live a fruitful and prosperous spiritual life.

A Biblical Path to Knowing God

When I sought God to understand how to abide, meditate, and cultivate His Word in my heart, I discovered guidance in Proverbs 2:1–5. While the entire chapter is a rich source of wisdom for seeking God, the first five verses provide an excellent starting point for anyone:

> *My son, if you accept my words, and store up my commandments within you—applying your ear to wisdom, inclining your heart to understanding—indeed, if you call out for discernment and raise your voice for insight—seeking it like silver and searching it out like hidden treasure—then you will understand the fear of the Lord and find the knowledge of God.*

Eight Stepping Stones to Spiritual Growth

There are at least eight essential stepping stones on this path, each designed to help you understand the fear of the Lord and find the knowledge of God. These steps describe a growing, personal relationship with Jesus Christ.

When you embrace these attitudes and actions, the promise of "then" from Proverbs 2:1–5 will manifest within you like a seed sprouting in good soil. This process of meditating on or abiding in God's Word is the work that He approves. It is how believers "labor into rest," by trusting God through obedience, demonstrating genuine faith.

9 Cultivating His Magnificent Promises

1. Accept His Words
God invites you to receive His promises as a child receives a father's love and assurances—with humility and trust. Listen attentively to what the Spirit is saying to you.

2. Store Up His Commandments
Treasuring God's Word requires intentionality. Memorize His promises- treasure His messages- storing them in your heart as a vital source of life and guidance. Just as you remember what is essential for daily living, so must you prioritize God's commandments. Deliberate focus and remembrance show respect for the One who speaks and reverence for His message.

3. Apply Your Ear to Wisdom
Listen closely to God's wisdom, tuning your ears as if trying to hear a single voice in a crowded room. True listening involves more than hearing—it leads to obedience. Loving God means giving Him your full attention, recognizing that His wisdom is for your benefit and growth.

4. Incline Your Heart to Understanding
Commit your heart and mind to grasping God's truth, allowing His Word to shape your thinking and transform your perspective. This requires a willingness to set aside your own judgments and trust in His infinite wisdom. Though you may not always comprehend immediately, persistence in seeking and believing will lead to deeper understanding.

5. Call Out for Discernment
Discernment is the ability to distinguish between good and evil, between selfish pride and humble obedience. Ever since Adam and Eve ate from the Tree of the Knowledge of Good and Evil, humanity has struggled with confusion, deception, and destruction due to a lack of understanding of what is truly good and evil. Pride undermines godly discernment, as it blinds and misleads. Without God opening your spiritual ears and eyes, discernment will elude you. Humbly pray for His guidance to gain true understanding.

We often associate crying with children and see calling for help as a sign of weakness. Yet, "the sacrifices of God are a broken spirit and a broken and crushed heart" (Psalm 51:17). The strong and proud never learn God's discernment because it requires humility. Crying to God reflects a deeper level of humility than we might be comfortable with, but the more broken we are before Him, the more earnestly our hearts will cry out. A broken heart and contrite Spirit are the offerings that please God. They draw the Heavenly Father near, allowing Him to teach you His ways and impart His discernment.

6. Raise Your Voice for Insight
The desire to understand and know God's ways is a journey, not a destination. It calls for a deep yielding to the Holy Spirit and trusting fully in His guidance. Gaining knowledge of the Holy One is an ongoing process of surrendering to God. Insight often comes through the process of learning by taking things apart and reassembling them again.

God may allow you to be figuratively taken apart during times of testing, trials, or suffering. These moments can feel like you're being dismantled to the very depths of your soul. Yet as you humbly turn to Him, the Spirit rebuilds you with wisdom, truth, and insight. This is reflected in Psalm 51:6, where King David humbles himself before the Lord and cries out, "I see you desire truth in the innermost being; and you teach me wisdom there."

Only the humble truly understand the ways of God, for He gives grace only to them. Lifting your voice is a humble, raw, and heartfelt cry for help, expressing your deep and sincere need for Him. It is through this brokenness that God imparts His wisdom and transforms your heart.

7. Seeking Wisdom like Silver
Wisdom is likened to silver, a precious and valuable treasure. Just as silver symbolizes redemption, God's wisdom is a priceless gift with the power to redeem and transform your life. Only the Spirit of God can reveal the immeasurable riches found in Christ's salvation. He is your Great Shepherd, your loving King, and the Lamb who was sacrificed for your reconciliation. May God's Spirit open your eyes to see and behold the Lamb of God who has taken away your sin!

8. Search for It like Hidden Treasure
Seeking God as a hidden treasure is an adventure, a journey fueled by intentionality and an intense desire to know Him. It's like setting out on a quest for a priceless treasure, with each step bringing you closer to the ultimate reward. To begin this journey, you must first believe that "anyone who would draw near to him must believe that he exists and that he rewards those who earnestly seek him" (Hebrews 11:6).

He is the treasure, and when you find Him, you will desire to sell all you have to purchase "the field" where the treasure is hidden (Matthew 13:44). The field represents the promises of God. Such intensity requires great grace, and as mentioned earlier, grace is given only to the humble. Yielding yourself to God as a living sacrifice is the ultimate act of humility. If you humbly search for Him through His promises, with sincere faith and a heart seeking Him, you will partake of His divine nature and receive everything that pertains to life and godliness.

Three "ifs" and One "Then"

"Then (*and only then*) you will understand the fear of the Lord and find the knowledge of God" (Proverbs 2:5, addition mine). Understanding the fear of the Lord comes through the actions and attitudes required by the three "ifs" mentioned above. The fear of the Lord is not merely an event or a fleeting feeling but a continual posture of brokenness and humility. This posture enables you to trust God as your Good Father and walk in His ways. "Humility is the fear of the Lord; its wages are riches and honor and life" (Proverbs 22:4 NIV).

When you live out the steps in Proverbs 2:1–5, you demonstrate true reverence and honor for God and His Word. The process itself manifests your fear, reverence, and love for the Lord. When you obey God out of genuine love for Him and His Word, you fulfill the commandment: "Love the LORD your God with all your heart and with all your soul and with all your strength" (Deuteronomy 6:5). Proverbs 2:1–5 prepares your heart to perceive the knowledge of the Holy One. Anything less than the intentional and consistent seeking of God is unworthy of the King and reveals a lack of understanding of who He is and who you are.

If you want to optimize your relationship with God, discern His magnificent and precious promises He has given you through His glory and goodness, and follow the commands of Proverbs 2:1–5. Do so with conviction, in step with the Holy Spirit's leading. If you find yourself lacking zeal to fulfill His Word, humbly cry out to God for wisdom and grace.

The Word of God Has Its Own Life

One way God has encouraged me to seek Him through His promises is by revealing the truth that His Word has its own life! Scripture declares that the Word of God is alive and powerful, carrying independent life and transformative power. These promises remind us that His Spirit, His very breath and life, is revealed and received through His Word. Such passages give insight into how the Spirit nourishes your inner being with God's eternal life.

Second Timothy 3:16–17 says, "All Scripture is inspired by God and is useful for teaching, for reproof, for correcting, and for training in righteousness so that the godly person may be complete, thoroughly equipped for every good work."

Now consider how this aligns with Hebrews 4:12–13:

For the word of God is living and active, sharper than any double-edged sword, piercing as far as the division of soul and spirit, and of joints, and marrow, able to judge the thoughts and attitudes of the heart. And there is no creature hidden from his sight; all things are uncovered and laid bare to the eyes of him to whom we must give account.

And again, Isaiah 55:10–11:

For just as the rain and snow come down from the sky and don't return there until they water the earth and make it fruitful and sprout crops, giving seed to the sower and food to the eater, so is my message when I speak it. It will not return to me unsuccessful. Rather, it will accomplish what I desire and succeed in the manner for which I sent it.

God's Word has its own life. "Let the word of Christ richly dwell within you " (Colossians 3:16). As you abide in Christ and His Word, it will grow and flourish within you.

The Path to Partaking in the Divine Nature

What I described in Proverbs 2:1–5 is part of the process of biblical meditation. In the Old Testament, the term *meditation* often means to contemplate or reflect deeply. It is similar to rumination, the process by which herbivores like cows digest their food. These animals have a multi-stomach digestive system, where food is repeatedly chewed, digested and returned to the mouth for further chewing. This process, known as "chewing the cud," ensures the full nourishment of the food.

This serves as a metaphor for how you can nourish your spiritual inner life. As Deuteronomy 8:3 reminds us, "People do not live by bread alone. Rather, they live by every word that comes from the mouth of the LORD." In the same way, you must receive, reflect on, and repeatedly contemplate God's promises as your spiritual nourishment.

Meditation involves intentionally musing on God's ways and thoughts over time, moving through distinct stages of deeper understanding. The art of meditating on God's Word is an essential spiritual discipline for every optimal disciple. Meditation and abiding are closely related. *Abiding* can be simply understood as "remembering and surrendering." To meditate or abide, you intentionally reflect on God's promises, actions, and character as revealed in Scripture. Then, in humble love, you surrender to that truth. This process of remembering and surrendering involves intentional reflection repeated over and over again.

Four Facets of My Bible Meditation

I use the following four steps to guide my meditation process as I "chew the cud" of God's messages. Consider this approach as a way to embrace abiding in Christ:

1. **Personalize**: I embrace every promise God gives me as a personal gift from Him. I receive it as a message of love from my heavenly Father. To personalize it, I insert my name as I read the passage, opening my spiritual ears to hear His thoughts and discern His ways. This approach deepens my connection with God and reminds me of His love for me.
2. **Harmonize**: As God's truth grows within me as a seed, I allow it to instruct, convict, correct, and train me in righteousness. Harmonizing involves walking in humility with an attitude of repentance and worship to align my heart and mind with His will. This process can include creating or reflecting on songs, poetry, or other expressions of worship. As Paul writes in 1 Corinthians 14:15, "I will pray with my Spirit, but I will also pray with my mind. I will sing praises with my spirit, but I will also sing with my mind." Harmonizing means yielding your whole being to God's truth and letting it shape you.
3. **Visualize:** I focus on seeing myself as God sees me, a new creation with a new identity in Christ. This transformational process empowers me to conform to the image of Christ. By visualizing God's perspective, I embrace my new identity, allowing my mind and attitudes to be transformed and renewed.
4. **Memorize**: Faithfully applying Proverbs 2:1–5 by meditating on and practicing the partaking of the divine nature through personalizing, harmonizing, and visualizing makes memorizing His magnificent promises much easier. Memorization solidifies His Word in my heart, making it an ever-present source of guidance and strength.

You Really Can Memorize Scripture

When teaching the memorization phase of the meditative or abiding process, I encourage using a word-for-word Bible translation (vs. a paraphrase) and committing to memorize each word exactly. Storing God's precious promises accurately is an essential discipline.

Often, the most resistance I encounter is towards this discipline of memorizing. The truth is, you can easily remember anything you use frequently. The human brain's capacity to learn and retain information is amazing, and the more you exercise this ability, the stronger and deeper it becomes. Memorization offers the unique gift of making God's promises readily available to you at any time, day or night. Remember, His Word is living and life-giving—it grows like a seed within you, even when you're not consciously focused on it. This powerful reality should encourage you to faithfully receive it, as it can transform even your subconscious mind.

While I emphasize abiding and meditation as powerful ways to cultivate God's promises within your inner being, other spiritual disciplines can also ingraft His Word into your life. I highly recommend Richard J. Foster's classic book *Celebration of Discipline: The Path to Spiritual Growth*. Foster identifies 12 spiritual disciplines, divided into three categories:

- **Inward Disciplines**: Meditation, Prayer, Fasting, and Study
- **Outward Disciplines**: Simplicity, Solitude, Submission, and Service
- **Corporate Disciplines**: Confession, Worship, Guidance, and Celebration

The Optimal Discipleship book focuses primarily on the Inward Disciplines to help you engraft God's promises into your soul and even your subconscious. However, the Holy Spirit can and will use all your humble, disciplined obedience to conform and transform you into the image and likeness of Christ. Seek Him to reveal to you how He has already been guiding you into disciplines of humility that *have previously enabled you* to partake of His divine nature. Remember, any experience of His presence is an opportunity to partake of that nature. Cultivate an awareness of His presence in your daily life.

If you desire an optimal spiritual life, receive His Word with love, store His commandments in your heart, and intentionally seek God through His promises and the disciplines He uses to disciple you. Humbly consider exploring the other spiritual disciplines Foster identifies, allowing the Holy Spirit to teach you His ways. Treating God and His Word with anything less than the utmost diligence and excellence is never a wise option.

For This Very Reason, Make Every Effort!

Let's reflect again on the apostle Peter's powerful call to action in 2 Peter 1:5–11, urging you to trust God's promises to produce Christ's life in you: "For this very reason, make every effort to add to your faith." Peter's insistence on making every effort to partake of the divine nature is not a suggestion; it is a command from God. The "divine nature" is God's Holy Spirit and refers to the character and attributes of God, which we are called to reflect in our lives.

Your spiritual vitality depends on actively participating in God's nature. Jesus invites us to abide in Him, to dwell in His presence, and to allow His Word to live richly in us. Through this discipline of abiding and meditating on His promises, you will add to your faith the character of Christ that you so deeply desire. Allow the Holy Spirit to breathe life into these words and awaken your soul through the whispers of His promises:

> *For this very reason, make every effort to add to your faith moral excellence; and to moral excellence, knowledge; and to knowledge, self-control; and to self-control, endurance; and to endurance, godliness; and to godliness, mutual affection; and to mutual affection, love. For if these qualities are in you and increasing, they will keep you from being ineffective and unproductive in your knowledge of our Lord Jesus Christ. For whoever does not have these qualities is blind—nearsighted, having forgotten that they received purification from their past sins. So, brothers and sisters, be diligent to make your calling and election firm, for by doing this you will never stumble; and this way you will receive a rich welcome into the eternal kingdom of our Lord and Savior Jesus Christ.*

Peter clearly understood that since God has provided everything you need for life and godliness and shown you *the path to access it,* there is no excuse not to pursue a diligent and intentional walk of obedience. You were created to be fruitful and multiply Christ's eternal life in this dying world—a mission that can only be accomplished by being formed in Christ as His Spirit lives and loves through you.

As we embark on our personal journeys of spiritual growth, we must ask ourselves: How can I recognize that Christ is being formed in me? What should I look for to reveal that I am cooperating with the Holy Spirit and becoming optimal in my relationship with God?

Now, step into the final chapter of *Optimal Disciple*: *Discovering How Christ Has Been Discipling You!* Its focus is to help you discern the evidence of God's life being formed in you as you believe and obey the insights Peter shares in 2 Peter 1. Scripture offers rich metaphors and images to encourage you along this journey. I pray these will inspire your faith, hope, and love as you walk in obedience!

CHAPTER 10

THE GARDEN HE DESIGNED FOR YOU.

(You were created to dwell in a garden, not a jungle.)

What no eye has seen, no ear has heard, no human mind has imagined, these are what God has prepared for those who love him.
1 CORINTHIANS 2:9

So far, in optimizing your relationship with our Lord and Savior Jesus Christ, you have focused on gaining insight into how He has been personally leading, discipling, and transforming you. From the beginning of your saving faith, He has been working to conform you to the image of His Son. Your obedience and maturity will manifest as you surrender to the Holy Spirit and intentionally yield to the process of sanctification through the magnificent personalized promises God has given you. This will result in you becoming more fruitful and productive in your service to Christ and others. As the Scripture reminds us, "Come near to God, and He will come near to you" (James 4:8).

God's purpose in intervening in your life through His indwelling Spirit is to live and love through you, bringing heaven into your life and extending it to the world around you. By faith, we pray, "May your kingdom come, and may your will be done, on earth as it is in heaven" (Matthew 6:10). Through your obedience, God can transform the jungle of your world into a garden of His grace.

As you understand from this book, abiding and dwelling in Christ is not a passive act but an intentional seeking of God through His promises.

This meditative and abiding process demonstrates your faith in the living God. Walking in the disciplines of His promises reveals your faith, but if you fail to do so continually, Scripture warns of spiritual withering. A withering faith is like a dry, brown leaf in autumn. As a child of God, if your faith begins to fade, God, in His love, will discipline you to draw you back to Him and prepare you for heaven. His discipline may involve leading you through fearful valleys, but His purpose in every trial is to conform you to the image of His Son.

Conformity may begin as an outside-in process, but true transformation always occurs from the inside-out. You can either learn this truth the hard way by neglecting the principles outlined in Peter's plan, your guide to spiritual growth, or humbly seek God through His promises. I pray you will follow Peter's plan and, with a humble heart, stay focused on Jesus Christ through the unique messages He has given you. Remember His way is gentle, His yoke is easy, and His burden is light (Matthew 11:30).

Proverbs 4:18–19 offers a simple yet profound glimpse into the path of transformation as you conform to the likeness of Christ. Reflect on these verses to gain insight into your future:

> *The way of the righteous is like the dawning light that shines brighter and brighter until full daylight. The way of the wicked is like darkness. They do not know what makes them stumble.*

As you partake of the divine nature, eternal life through Jesus Christ, and the essence of the Spirit of God, you will be transformed from the inside out, just as Jesus was transfigured before Peter, James, and John. This promise of transformation should fill you with hope and inspiration. While you may not physically glow, your life will radiate Christ's light, dispersing the darkness of the world through your character and behavior.

As you continue your journey in Christ, His Word will illuminate your path, making it clearer and your stumbling less frequent. Truly, His Word will become a "lamp to guide [your] feet, a light on [your] path" (Psalm 119:105). It will not only guide you but also reassure and shape you as it transforms your character, enabling you to reflect Christ more fully. Through His Word, you'll find both direction in this life and preparation for the heavenly home He has promised.

God Reveals Transformation through Creation and His Word

How do the Scriptures and creation describe what you are meant to become as you grow in your faith and impact your world? What transformation does God desire to manifest through you?

Some of God's most amazing examples of transformation come from creation itself. From the very beginning, God revealed His nature and power through the act of creation. If you remember and restore your confidence in Him as the Creator, you'll see that He designed this world through His spoken word. In Genesis 1, we read, "God said," yet how often do we pause to ponder that Christ Jesus created everything by His words? He continues to develop, sustain, and control all things through the power of His spoken word. Hebrews 1:3 reveals that Jesus Christ "is the radiance of God's glory, is the exact representation of his nature, and sustains all things by His powerful word."

When you seek God through intentional and disciplined abiding in His promises, you metaphorically pour the new wine of the divine nature into the old wineskins of your present life. Jesus speaks to this process in Matthew 9:16–17:

> *No one puts a patch of unshrunk cloth on a tear in an old garment, because the patch will pull away from the garment, making the tear worse. Nor does anyone put new* (i.e., unaged) *wine into old wineskins—for the skins will burst, the wine will pour out, and the skins will be ruined. Rather, they put new wine into new wineskins, and both are preserved.*

This illustrates that transformation in your life is inevitable when you abide in Christ. Expect positive changes in your attitudes, behavior, and even your health. But also be prepared for old things to pass away; just like an old wineskin is replaced by a new one. However, keep in mind that changes will be in God's timing, in God's way, and for His glory, not yours. And when others notice your transformation and growth, be sure to give all the glory to Him!

10 *The Garden He Designed for You*

Transformation from the Inside-Out

In Chapter 6, the transformative journey of the caterpillar was briefly introduced as a metaphor for spiritual growth. Now, we'll delve deeper into this incredible process, drawing parallels between the caterpillar's metamorphosis into a butterfly and the profound transformation God works within us as we abide in Him and embrace His promises.

The butterfly begins its life as a small, seed-like egg that hatches into worm-like caterpillar, crawling on many legs and consuming everything it can to grow rapidly. Then, at a specific moment, triggered by its internal design, the caterpillar instinctively knows it must stop its previous activities. It finds a secure twig to cling to and begins an incredible transformation. Inside the chrysalis it weaves, the caterpillar's body is completely dissolved, and every aspect of its physical form is recreated.

The ground-crawling worm ceases to exist. In its place, a new creation emerges, complete with delicate wings, slender legs, and powerful muscles for flight. This once-earthbound creature now soars to heights it could never have imagined as a caterpillar.

During the chrysalis stage, when the butterfly's DNA transforms a crawling caterpillar into a flying insect, the caterpillar must essentially "die" to allow the recreation process to fulfill its designed purpose. This is a perfect example of an inside-out transformation. Keep this in mind as you practice the disciplines of ingesting the promises and messages God has spoken into your heart. These disciplines, when humbly maintained, create the space for metamorphosis to occur. However, only the Holy Spirit can transform your heart, soul, mind, and body to become Christlike, enabling you to partake of the divine nature to fulfill God's optimal design for you. Fix your spiritual eyes on Jesus Christ and abide in Him, comparing yourself only to Him, not to others.

Another dramatic illustration from creation that serves as a metaphor for spiritual development is the frog. Like the butterfly, it begins its life from a seed-like egg. Born in the water, the tadpole is like a fish, yet it must be transformed into an air-breathing adult frog that lives on land, hopping and moving on legs. While the butterfly undergoes a complete dissolving and reorganization of its physical being, the frog's metamorphosis is more gradual. Its transformation unfolds slowly, in plain sight, offering a different yet equally profound picture of conforming change.

The frog, as an amphibian, lives in two environments—water and land. This reveals a metaphorical truth about us as believers: we, too, inhabit two realms. You were physically born into natural life, but through Christ, you have been spiritually reborn into God's eternal life. Until you pass from this natural life, you will navigate both natures. Just as the frog thrives in water and on land, you are called to sit in heavenly places while walking in the Spirit in this world.

These two illustrations from creation emphasize the essential truth that your transformation always begins from the inside out. As you humbly submit to God's Word in loving obedience, your metamorphosis will unfold according to His design and providential timing, not yours.

Beautiful Spiritual Gardens Bear Beautiful Fruit

The apostles Paul and Peter both provide lists of the qualities and fruit that describe the growing, maturing, and optimal follower of Christ—manifested by God's power working from the inside out. When combining the lists in Galatians 5:22 and 2 Peter 1:5-7, the qualities and fruit of the Spirit can be described as:

- Love
- Joy
- Peace
- Patience
- Self-Control
- Endurance
- Kindness
- Goodness
- Gentleness
- Moral Excellence
- Knowledge
- Godliness
- Faithfulness or Steadfastness
- Mutual Affection

10 The Garden He Designed for You

Peter teaches that these qualities of Christ and the fruit of the Spirit will increase as we partake of the divine nature. Therefore, if you humbly walk in the discipline of your promises, it is expected that the Holy Spirit will form Christ in you.

As you participate in the divine nature, your thinking begins to align more closely with Christ's, and you gain the grace to behave as a beloved child of God. Scripture presents several metaphoric and organic illustrations to reveal what God promises to accomplish *in and through* anyone who diligently seeks Him. Let's explore these images to better understand what an optimal, growing disciple of the Lord should embody.

Meditator Blessings: Becoming a Strong and Healthy Fruit Tree

Psalm 1:3 beautifully portrays the meditating person as "like a tree planted by streams of water that yields its fruit in season, and whose leaf does not wither. Whatever that person does prospers." The thriving tree represents the life of someone who delights in and meditates on the Lord's Word. In contrast, the wicked, who do not meditate on God, are described as "like the chaff that the wind drives away."

The two individuals in Psalm 1 are dramatically different. The righteous delight in God's Word and prosper spiritually, while the wicked reject His guidance, withering without fruit. Their endings are vastly different: "Therefore, the wicked will not have standing in the judgment, nor sinners in the assembly of the righteous. For the LORD knows the way of the righteous, but the way of the wicked will perish" (Psalm 1:5).

The Bible describes the righteous person as fruitful and prosperous. These words reflect an optimal, flourishing life—not in terms of material gain but in spiritual vitality. While integrity and honorable living may open doors to earthly favor and blessings, the true prosperity here is rooted in a life that abides in God's promises and reflects His eternal purposes. The more honorable life a person lives, the more opportunities they have, and the more they can acquire the favor of people and material blessings.

The Fruitfulness of Abiding in Christ and His Word

John 15:1–17 paints a vivid picture of the fruitful life as one that abides continually in the True Vine—Jesus Christ, the source of all spiritual life and nourishment for his followers. "If you abide in me, and my words abide in you, ask whatever you wish, and it will be done for you. By this my Father is glorified, that you bear much fruit and so prove to be my disciples" (John 15:7–8 ESV).

However, for those who do not abide, the outcome is starkly different: "If anyone does not abide in me he is thrown away like a branch and withers, and the branches are gathered, thrown into the fire, and burned" (John 15:6 ESV). These two paths—fruitful life or spiritual withering—diverge at the decision to abide in Christ and meditate on His Word. Without abiding, internal faith wanes, external obedience falters, and the connection to the life-giving Vine is lost.

In John 15:1–17, Jesus promises extraordinary blessings for those who abide: fruitfulness, friendship with Him, answered prayers, the fullness of His joy, assurance of Christ choosing you, and the ability to love as He loves. This fruitful abundance reflects the optimal life God intends for His disciples—one of deep communion with Christ that glorifies the Father and reveals His love to the world.

The Righteous Finish Strong

Psalm 92:12–15 uses rich organic metaphors to illustrate the strength and fruitfulness of the righteous (those who intentionally seek God, even into their old age):

> *The righteous will flourish like a palm tree; they will grow like the cedars of Lebanon. Those who are planted in the house of the LORD will flourish in the courts of our God. They will bear fruit in old age, still green and full of sap. They will declare, "The LORD is upright; He is my rock, and there is no unrighteousness in him."*

Date palms adorned the walls of Moses' tabernacle and Solomon's Temple, symbolizing that fruitfulness thrives in the presence of God. This imagery reminds us that when we dwell in the house of the Lord, we too will flourish.

Notice that Scripture doesn't compare spiritual growth to the rapid growth of banana trees, but rather to the steady, long-term growth of palm trees and the majestic cedars of Lebanon. This shows that spiritual growth—like the journey from seed to fruit—is not a quick process. However, the more you intentionally seek God through His personal promises, the more you can accelerate this process and experience the fullness of His presence and kingdom.

Your fruitfulness is evidence of God's transformative work in you and through you, turning a wilderness of faithlessness into a garden of His grace. As you bear the fruit, your life proclaims the truth of Philippians 2:13: "God who works in you to will and to work for his good pleasure."

The Power of Your *Personal* Message from God

The prophet Isaiah provides one of the clearest depictions of the impact of receiving and responding to God's promises for those who make Him their priority. At the end of Isaiah 55, The Lord reveals the beauty of a life yoked to Him in holy discipline and nourished by His Word:

> *For just as the rain and the snow come down from the sky and don't return there until they water the earth and make it fruitful and sprout crops, giving seed to the sower and food to the eater, so is my message when I speak it. It will not return to me unsuccessful. Rather, it will accomplish what I desire and succeed in the matter for which I sent it. For you will go out with joy and be led out with peace. The mountains and hills will break forth with a joyful shout before you. All the trees of the countryside will clap their hands. The juniper will come up instead of the thornbush, and the myrtle instead of the stinging nettle. This will be for the* Lord's *fame, an everlasting sign that will never be cut off* (Isaiah 55:10–13).

Through this prophetic vision, Isaiah provides organic metaphors of nature to reveal profound spiritual truths. God's Word and Spirit, like nourishing rain, are meant to sustain you, causing His life within you to bring forth and sprout. Just as natural seeds sprout to reproduce and nourish others, so too does God's Word equip you, "giving seed to the sower and food to the eater." His purpose is to fill you with His life and grace so that you can share His truth with the spiritually hungry around you.

It is crucial that this life-giving Word comes from God, full of Spirit and truth, rather than from your own will or efforts. The Holy Spirit must provide the message or promise, and when it is truly from Him, it will be evidenced by the peace and joy that follow: "You will go out with joy and be led out with peace." Even the "mountains and the hills"—the challenges and obstacles you face—"will break forth with a joyful shout." This signifies that God will grant you the grace and wisdom to see difficulties as opportunities to praise and trust Him, allowing Christ to be formed in you.

Your growing faith and deepening knowledge will humble you, giving you the grace to rest in the peace that He is sovereign over all things. This confidence will inspire others, as "all the trees of the countryside (God's true children) will clap their hands" (addition mine) in celebration of your faithfulness and service to the King. Your trust in God will reveal His grace to others and encourage them to walk in faith.

Isaiah goes on to declare how God's transforming work reverses the curse, turning a spiritual jungle into a flourishing garden: "The juniper will come up instead of the thornbush and the myrtle instead of the stinging nettle." Where once there was bitterness and pain, beauty and goodness will grow. Your life, transformed by God's promises, will honor Him and "this will be for the Lord's fame, an everlasting sign that will never be cut off."

Spiritual Prosperity and Success

It is no surprise that the Lord tells Joshua in Joshua 1 that meditating on God's Word and promises will lead to spiritual prosperity and success. The Bible consistently emphasizes the blessings of an abundantly fruitful life for those who intentionally meditate on and abide in God's Word and character. I encourage you to explore Scripture for this vital discipline, one that God desires to teach each of His children. He longs to reveal Himself to you and to all who trust in His Son. Ultimately, His work in you is to transform you into the image of His beloved Son, enabling you to fully enjoy the garden of His grace.

So, what is your destiny? While God's ultimate plans for your life many not yet be fully clear, you can be certain that no one comprehends the full scope of their fruitfulness before He reveals it to them. In heaven, you will be amazed to see the eternal impact of your earthly obedience. Your responsibility now is to walk in the Spirit, yoked to His promises, so that you may become a profitable servant to your Master and King. This is the highest and noblest life you can live, adorned by His grace.

This life will reflect what Jesus is doing right now in heaven: praying for the lost and broken, interceding for the expansion of His kingdom in the hearts and minds of people. Whatever your role or calling may be, it will all be for God's glory because Christ will be your all and all. As an optimal disciple, your heart's motto will echo John the Baptist's (a very optimal follower of God) humble response to Jesus, "He must become greater, and I must become less" (John 3:30).

As you yield to God's grace, obey His Word, and learn to rest and abide in the shadow of His wings, your life will become an offering of love and sacrifice to the King. You will witness His garden of grace transforming your world with His glorious presence.

EPILOGUE

WHAT DIFFERENCE DOES IT MAKE?

Before you close this book, I pray you will take a moment to ask yourself an important question: *What difference does viewing spiritual formation through Peter's path make in my life, and how does it impact how I make disciples?*

Work Out the Salvation That God Has Worked In

If you've grasped the principles in this book, you now understand the biblical process of spiritual growth and formation, as described in 2 Peter 1, begins within your inner being. Your mind and soul are transformed by God's Spirit through His promises, given when you encounter His glory and goodness, and engraft them through inward and outward disciplines.

The process of Christ being formed in you started when you placed your faith in Him. At that moment, through His righteousness, you were transferred from the domain of darkness into the kingdom of God. You also know that your promises are unique, personal messages from your heavenly Father. They were given to you when you encountered the glory and virtue of Christ as He called you to Himself. It is through these great and magnificent promises that you may partake of the divine nature.

God's Spirit enables you to add to your faith the virtues of Christ through inward, outward and corporate disciplines. This is the path for manifesting the spiritual characteristics of Christ and impacting your world with truth and grace. Your spiritual formation begins with an encounter with Christ and is revealed through your faithful obedience, allowing the Holy Spirit to live and love through you.

Because this process is uniquely personal, it calls for a shift in how we approach disciple-making. Rather than focusing on telling others how to follow Christ, we should ask questions that encourage them to share how Christ has already been discipling them. Through His promises, how has Jesus Christ empowered them to grow in their disciplines of humble faithfulness and obedience to Him?

Paul wrote in Colossians 2:6–7, "Therefore walk in Christ Jesus the Lord, just as you have received Him and just as you were taught, firmly rooted, built up in him, established in the faith, and overflowing with thanksgiving." However, with the best intentions, this passage has often been misinterpreted by leaders to mean, "Therefore walk in Christ Jesus the Lord, *as I (the leader/disciple-maker) have received Him* and just as you were taught *(according to what is acceptable in our brand of Churchanity)*, firmly rooted, built up in him, established in the faith, and overflowing with thanksgiving" (my paraphrase). I know this happens because I've done it myself—with the best of motives and the support of the discipling literature I've read.

This confusion of attempting transformation from the outside in is vividly expressed by Paul in Galatians 3:2–3, "The only thing I wish to learn from you is this: Did you receive the Holy Spirit by works of the law or by hearing the gospel with faith? Are you so foolish to think that after beginning your walk of faith through the work of the Holy Spirit, you are now being perfected by unspiritual means?" The "unspiritual means" are anything that separates you from depending on the power of the Holy Spirit, which you receive through partaking of the divine nature of Christ. Remember, you partake of, or participate in, the divine nature through the personalized promise(s) He has given you. That is what makes your relationship with God truly *personal!*

Your walk in Christ requires constant surrender and humble reliance on Him. This dependence on Father God should guide every step of your journey. The Scriptures instruct you to "humbly receive the word *(messages of promise received through His glory and goodness)* implanted in you *(and cultivated through abiding in His Word),* which can save your souls" (James 1:21, additions mine).

Most of the discipleship training methods and spiritual formation books I have observed bypass the critical process of identifying and abiding in or meditating on the unique promises given to each believer by Jesus Christ. Your promises form your personal pathway to partake of Christ. To cooperate with the Holy Spirit in forming Christ in someone, you cannot step between Christ and those He has redeemed! Mature and optimal disciples live out their convictions of faith that God revealed to them through His glory and goodness, not through pride or human willpower. That distinction is crucial in understanding the difference between cooperating with the Spirit's work and teaching reliance on fleshly efforts and the wisdom of this world.

It's time for followers of Jesus Christ to consistently be led by the Holy Spirit through an internal love relationship with Him. As you understand and live out the process of Peter's path through Spirit-led disciplines, you will experience greater freedom in Christ and be better equipped to lead others into that same freedom.

Do You Trust God Enough to Do It His Way?

- Do you *truly believe* you care more about doing God's will than His Spirit, who dwells in you?
- Do you think you care more about reaching people for Christ than the Savior who gave His life for them?

The church will become more effective in its mission when more members of Christ's body allow the Holy Spirit to lead them in sharing the gospel. While we have a clear command to preach the gospel to all the world and make disciples, every step must be taken under the power and leadership of the Spirit of Christ our King.

Peter gave us a clear path to follow: "For this very reason . . . add to your faith" *(to produce the fruit and qualities that prove you are His disciples)*, "for if these qualities are in you and increasing, they will keep you from being ineffective and unproductive in the knowledge of our Lord Jesus Christ" (2 Peter 1:5, 8). The more we know the Lord and partake of his divine nature, the more passion and zeal we will have to do his will!

My prayer for the body of Christ is that we will humbly follow the many Scriptures that call us to renew our first love, daily nurturing our unique, personal relationship with Him and living out our convictions to follow Christ Jesus closely.

May God deepen your relationship with Him as you discover how He has been discipling you, so you may allow the Disciple Maker, Christ Jesus, to disciple others through you and draw people to Father God.

God bless you,
Pastor Neil DeSiato

DISCOVERY QUESTIONS

The following questions are designed to guide personal or group discussions, helping you gain a deeper understanding of how Christ has been disciplining you. Ideally, these discussions would take place in a small group of two to five trusted Christ followers who are willing to embark on this journey with you.

Suggestions for the process:

- **Prepare**: Each group member should secure a copy of *Optimal Disciple* and read it at least once. Before starting, review the questions to focus your mind on key themes as you read.
- **Engage**: Before the first meeting, take time to thoughtfully read and answer all the questions for the chapter being studied. Ideally, work through the book sequentially, as the material builds on earlier chapters.
- **Leadership**: Designate a group leader or facilitator who can guide the discussion, keep the group on track, and ensure everyone has an opportunity to share. This person should be someone who is mature in their faith and skilled at fostering an open and supportive environment.
- **Discuss**: Plan for a 1–2 hour session to allow ample time for everyone to share their unique insights, thoughts, and struggles in their spiritual formation. Each person's perspective is valuable and contributes to the group's growth.

Chapter 1
Our Unique Journeys into Christ Jesus

1. Paraphrase "the gospel" as defined by Paul in 1 Corinthians 15:1.
2. List the new covenant spiritual blessings given to all who believe in Jesus Christ.
3. What is the mission of everyone who believes in Jesus Christ?
4. Colossians 2:6–7 says, "Therefore walk in Christ Jesus the Lord, just as you have received Him and just as you were taught." How did you receive Christ? How does that unique experience impact the way you live out your faith?
5. Baptism represents humbly dying to self. What does humility mean to you? What disciplines do you practice to grow in your humility towards God?
6. How do *you* practice letting Jesus live through you (Galatians 2:20)?
7. Since "teaching them to observe everything that I have commanded you" (Matthew 28:20) in the Great Commission includes God's unique and personal instructions to you, how might this change the way you witness to others?
8. Explain the two parts of God's command: "to walk humbly with God and to love others as He loves you" (Micah 6:8; John 13:34).
9. As you strive to be yoked to the promises of God, what are some Scriptures that have given you spiritual rest or peace? How do they help you stay focused on God's purpose for your life?
10. When has the Holy Spirit taken apart a biblical truth and built it into your heart?

Chapter 2
The Blueprint for Becoming an Optimal Disciple: The New Covenant

1. In your own words, summarize the seven promises God gave us through the prophets Jeremiah and Ezekiel.
2. Why was there a need for a new covenant?
3. How does the promise "I will forgive their wrongdoing and remember their sins no more" (Hebrews 8:12) impact your daily life and relationships with others?
4. Which new covenant promises touched your heart the most when you first came to faith in Christ?
5. Which new covenant promises impact you the most?
6. True or false: The new covenant is the blueprint for everything God destined through the work of Christ's life, death, burial, and resurrection. Explain your answer.
7. What are some ways the new covenant has changed the way you interact with others?
8. How should the new covenant impact your conversation when sharing the gospel or when encouraging someone to walk more closely with Jesus?
9. How does this approach to growing spiritually differ from the typical Christian discipleship training you've received in the past?

Chapter 3
Peter's Path to an Optimal Life

Read 2nd Peter 1

1. How does Peter's motivation in writing this letter apply to you (vv.12–15)?
2. List the four progressive truths in verses 3–4. The first one is a statement, and the other three begin with the word "through."
3. How does Peter describe the process for believers to "add to their faith" (vv. 3–5)?
4. Why is Peter insistent that "these qualities are in you and increasing" (vv. 8–9)?
5. How do you describe God's glory?
6. How do you describe God's goodness, virtue, or excellence?
7. How is Paul's conversion in Acts 9 a pattern of Peter's path revealed in 2 Peter 1?
8. How did God's glory and goodness draw you to Him?
9. What new covenant promises has the Holy Spirit revealed as your personal promises from God (v. 4)?
10. How have your promises become a light to guide your path (Psalm 119:105)?
11. Since God has given you all you need to live a godly life, what disciplines do you practice to *partake* of His divine nature through the promises He has given you (vv. 3–4)?
12. What do we gain by adding to our faith (v. 8)?
13. What does it say about us when we are not partaking of His divine nature or adding to our faith (v. 9)?
14. How do you "make your calling and election firm," and how does it benefit you (vv. 10–11)?
15. Compare 2 Peter 1:3–4 and Hebrews 3:12–14. What are your takeaways from these verses?

Chapter 4
Discerning Your Promise(s): The Gifts from His Glory and Goodness

1. When did you first recognize the Lord Jesus Christ calling you to trust Him for peace in your soul? What were the circumstances?
2. What promises did you believe when you placed your trust in Christ?
3. Peter writes that those who trust God's promises in Christ "received a faith of the same kind as" his own faith in Christ. This means we have access to the same power as all faithful followers of God, with everything we need to live a faithful, joyful, and blessed life. Why do you think many Christ followers don't live up to their God-given potential?
4. The Holy Spirit revealed through Peter's letter that we were given "Magnificent and precious promises." When did this happen in your life? What two words does Peter use to describe God's action during your encounter with Him?
5. How do you describe or understand the glory and goodness of God? How have you experienced it? How do you continue to encounter His Spirit?
6. Why is it important to discern and meditate on the great and precious promises God has given you?
7. How did Peter, James, and John respond to witnessing the transfiguration of Jesus? How did it impact Peter's thinking and transform his life?
8. Can you identify one or two other biblical figures who experienced God's glory and goodness? How did it impact them? What changes did they make or acts of obedience did they perform? (Hint: Isaiah 6; Acts 9)
9. Do you recall moments in your life when God's presence was undeniably real? How did His presence, glory, and goodness impact and change you?
10. Reflecting on the previous question, what verse or promise did God impress upon your heart during that time? Was there a new understanding of God that became a guiding lamp and light

in your walk with Christ (Psalm 119:105)? Do you remember receiving a specific promise of faith, hope, or love (Psalm 119:49)?
11. How have you responded to the promises God has given you? Have you planted them in your heart and nurtured them with joy, praise, and thanksgiving? Explain how your life might change if you intentionally cultivate the great and precious promises personally given to you by Jesus Christ. How can you discipline your mind to seek the Lord and fully embrace His promises?

Chapter 5
How God Prepared the Soil of Your Soul to Become an Optimal Disciple

Read Psalm 139, focusing on verses 13–18.

1. What is the overarching theme of this psalm? Consider how the opening (v. 1) and closing (vv. 23–24) thoughts connect.
2. Verses 13–18 reveal the intricate and sequential progression of our physical, mental, emotional, and spiritual development—written long before the discovery of DNA or modern understanding of human growth in the womb. How would you describe each step of this process?
3. Jesus often used the imagery of soil and seeds in His parables to reveal spiritual truths. Can you identify two to three Bible passages where God's people are compared to a garden, soil, planting, vine, or another organic metaphor?
4. Psalm 139:13 highlights how God knows our identity, purpose, and deepest passions far better than we know ourselves. Are there any Bible passages that resonate with your sense of identity and purpose? How did you come to connect with them?
5. Psalm 139:14 reflects themes found in Psalm 100.
- Genuine worship is always rooted in humility and spiritual dependence on God.
- Read Psalm 100:1–6 and reflect on how His creation of your entire being and your purpose inspires worship in you.
6. Psalm 139:15 emphasizes the unique characteristics God has intentionally given you. List some traits you appreciate about yourself and others you might struggle with. Does knowing that God personally chose these features change how you view yourself? Please explain your response.
7. Psalm 139:16; Ephesians 2:10; and Romans 8:28–30 reveal that God formed a providential plan for you, establishing your destiny to do good works even before you were born. Does this truth encourage or discourage you as you reflect on your personal history? How has it impacted your confidence in doing God's will?

8. Is it clear that God has been leading you to fulfill the purpose He designed for you? How do your unique, distinguishing traits complement your God-given purpose?
9. Psalm 139:17–18 reveals that God's constant outpouring of love, grace, and assurance is like sunlight streaming down to sustain life on Earth. What are some of His gracious thoughts that strengthen you daily? If you could "catch a sunbeam" of His love and hold onto it for a rainy day (difficult times), how would it help you? How are you responding to the Sonshine of His constant, precious thoughts toward you?
10. How have God's precious thoughts become a lamp and light to guide your daily path (Psalm 119:105)?
11. Paraphrase Psalm 139:13–18 in your own words:
12. What action steps will you take based on the truths revealed in these verses?

Chapter 6
Key Attitudes and Insights of an Optimal Disciple

1. Why is your attitude towards God and His Word essential to becoming an optimal disciple?
2. How do your attitudes influence your choices? How has your attitude towards God or an authority figure positively or negatively impacted your life?
3. What evidence of the fruit of the Spirit do you see in your life? How have others affirmed your spiritual growth in the qualities described in 2 Peter 1:5–7?
4. In your own words, list the seven attitudes essential for becoming an optimal disciple.
5. When did you first surrender your heart and mind to the lordship of Jesus Christ?
6. How do you demonstrate your submission towards God? What practices in your life reveal your love for Him above all else?
7. Why were the Thessalonians growing strong in their faith in Christ? How did their attitude towards God's Word contribute to their growth? Compare their attitude to that of the believers described in Hebrews 5:11–14.
8. How does understanding God's agenda change how you face challenges, suffering, and disappointment?
9. What is the difference between good and evil and right and wrong?
10. How have you developed discernment between good and evil? Why do people naturally lack spiritual discernment?
11. How is virtue developed in your life? How does discipline contribute to the freedom you experience?
12. What are some of the devil's schemes that try to derail your focus on Jesus and your growth?
13. Which attitude do you believe is most essential for your spiritual growth? Why?
14. What other attitudes do you think should be included as essential for becoming an optimal disciple?
15. How do the essential questions in chapter 6 help keep you focused on Jesus and His unique promises for you?

16. In what ways does Psalm 84 reveal the essential attitudes and behaviors of an optimal disciple?
17. How does following the guidance in 2 Peter 1 produce these essential attitudes in a believer's life?

Chapter 7
How Do the Magnificent and Precious Promises Become a Light to Your Path?

1. Why does God give us His promises? Please write out 2 Peter 1:3–4 in your own words.
2. How can we know we are participating in His divine nature? What attitude is essential to begin the process?
3. Ephesians 5:17 urges to "not be foolish but understand what the will of the Lord is." How does the Bible describe God's will for you? Consider Romans 8:28–30 and 12:1–2.
4. Please paraphrase Romans 8:28–30 in your own words.
5. Please paraphrase Romans 12:1–2 in your own words.
6. What is the key question we should ask in every problem, trial, or struggle we face?
7. What metaphors does the Bible use to describe God's Word? Which of these metaphors resonate with your life?
8. When do we receive God's magnificent and precious promises?
9. What are common ways people respond to a promise or word from God? Reflect on the Parable of the Sower in Matthew 13 as you consider your answer.
10. How did God's promise in John 15:16 change the Author's life? What verse has done the same for you?
11. What period of the Author's life was most impacted by these promises? How does your story compare?
12. When have you experienced a similar process in your life where a promise from God expanded your understanding of His character?
13. How have the promises God has given you empowered you to grow in Christlikeness?
14. What are some ways you nurture and cultivate God's promises in your soul?

Chapter 8
The God of Your Promises

1. Why is it important to understand that God has *always* related to humanity through personalized messages and promises? How might this knowledge deepen your trust in His Word and His plans for your life?
2. How does Psalm 119 help you understand how God has related to humanity through promises?
3. How does the use of the word "promise" when referring to a message from God differ from words like *laws, commandments, rules, statutes, precepts, paths, or testimonies*? How does your response to a promise compare to your response to a rule?
4. Why is it important to understand where and when transforming messages (i.e., promises) were given to each biblical character? Reread 2 Peter 1:3–4. When did you receive a promise from God? Why is it ineffective to try to come up with your own personal promises?
5. Why is it essential to embrace the unique promises tied to your identity *and* abide by them as God describes in Isaiah 55:10–11?
6. How does recognizing God's consistent use of personalized messages (i.e., promises) deepen your reverence for Him and His Word?
7. Choose any biblical character. How did they respond to God's promises? How did their obedience or disobedience affect their covenant with God? (For example, think of King David and King Saul.)
8. Define the word *covenant*. How do the unique promises you receive from God form a covenant between you and your heavenly Father, allowing you to partake of His divine nature?
9. Reflect on the promises God made throughout the Bible. Did the people recorded in Scripture understand the implications of these promises? How should this influence our perception of the promises we receive? (Refer to John 14:12.)

10. What is the one constant behavior humanity has displayed throughout history? What is the one constant behavior God has displayed? What does this tell you about yourself and about God?
11. Why does God remain unwaveringly committed to His covenant with humanity? (Hint: Ezekiel 36:16–17.)
12. What role does Jesus Christ play in God's promises to us? What is our responsibility in this divine arrangement? (Hint: 2 Corinthians 1:20.)
13. Why is the new covenant the most wonderful covenant ever given to humanity?

Preface to Chapters 9 and 10

1. Why do you think the author wrote the preface to chapters 9 and 10?
2. The author shared a transformative encounter with the Holy Spirit after meditating on Psalm 139. When have you experienced a similar encounter with God that profoundly altered your perspective about yourself or Him?
3. Even though the author had a life-changing experience, what do you think he didn't fully understand about the epiphany and the personal message he received from God?
4. What should he have continued to do with Psalm 139? What do you think caused the author to drift away from God, even though he was actively serving in church work and helping others?
5. How did the Lord help restore the author's mind and heart at the wedding chapel? What are your thoughts on this experience?
6. How do you think the author could have started two churches yet confess that during that time he didn't understand how to guide others into spiritual formation?
7. How did God use the book *Sacred Marriage* in the author's life?
8. What do you think the author meant when he wrote, "My spiritual life resembled the Israelites in the book of Judges rather than the victories described in the book of Joshua"?
9. What was the author missing in his understanding of the process of making a disciple or helping others understand their spiritual formation?
10. Isaiah 55 was enormously powerful in the author's life, yet it didn't directly impact the congregation he pastored. Why do you think it had such a different effect on him than on his congregation?
11. How important is it to lead people the way the Holy Spirit is leading them? How could failing to do this contribute to spiritual burnout for a pastor or congregation?
12. How did the Holy Spirit lead the author to discover the personal connection to spiritual formation in 2 Peter 1?

13. Why do you think the author believes 2 Peter 1 reveals a clear understanding of how to be an optimal follower of Christ?
14. Considering 2 Peter 1, what does God desire for each of His children?

Chapter 9
Cultivating His Magnificent Promises

1. In your journey towards becoming optimal in your walk with Christ, you may have discerned one or more of God's great and precious promises. Which promise(s) do you want to cultivate and engraft into your heart, mind, soul, and body?
2. James 1:21 says, "Humbly receive the word implanted (engrafted) in you, which can save you, which can save your souls" (addition mine). What does a humble attitude towards God and His word look like in action?
3. How does the Virgin Mary's story in Luke 1:26–38 illustrate the way we should also conceive God's life in us?
4. Our spiritual journeys always begin with an intervention from God. Many times, He uses our needs to make us realize our dependence on Him and His Word. What concerns or circumstances did you face when God planted a precious promise in your heart?
5. How have God's precious promises influenced the way you identify yourself?
6. How is cultivating God's Word (seed) in your life similar to a gardener tending a garden?
7. How are the concepts of "mediating on Scripture" and "abiding in Christ" similar? (Refer to Psalm 1:3 and John 15:6.)
8. Consider Proverbs 2:1–5 as a cultivation plan or guide for developing habits and disciplines that allow the Holy Spirit to produce His fruit in your life. What do these verses teach?
9. Explain why Proverbs 2:5 says that when we act on and live out the truths of verses 1–4, we will "understand the fear of the Lord and find the knowledge of God."
10. Since the Word of God has its own life, how might that life impact your own? (Refer to Hebrews 4:12–13 and 2 Timothy 3:16–17.)
11. God created herbivores with four stomachs, a metaphor for the process of meditation. Describe four ways you can personally digest God's Word.
12. Have you discovered additional ways to participate and partake of God's divine nature?

Chapter 10
The Garden He Designed for You

(You were created to dwell in a garden, not a jungle.)

1. How would you describe your spiritual life? Is it more like a garden or a jungle? Why do you think this is true?
2. What has changed in your life as you've gained understanding of how God has personally led, discipled, and transformed you?
3. Read the following quote from the book and explain how you've seen this happening in your own life: "Your obedience and maturity will manifest as you surrender to the Holy Spirit and intentionally yield to the process of sanctification through the magnificent promises God has given you. This will result in you becoming more fruitful and productive in your service to Christ and others."
4. Since experiencing saving faith, what promise of God has been the most transformative in leading you to conform to the image of His Son (Romans 8:29)?
5. The author used organic metaphors to describe spiritual growth and maturity. In what ways did this approach improve your understanding?
6. In Psalm 1, the contrast is drawn between the prospering, meditating person and the withering, wicked one. What are your thoughts on the idea of an "in-between" spiritual place for Christians?
7. Psalm 1 describes meditation as a key to optimizing spiritual growth, while John 15 emphasizes abiding. Are these concepts the same, or do you see a difference? Please explain.
8. How does the metaphor of the date palm tree in Psalm 92:12–15 inspire hope for your spiritual growth?
9. Philippians 2:13 says, "God who works in you to will and to work for his good pleasure." How does this verse encourage or challenge you in your spiritual growth?
10. In Joshua 1, the Lord tells Joshua that meditating on God's Word will bring spiritual prosperity and success. How have you found

this to be true in your life? What have you meditated on, and how has it changed you?
11. What passages from Psalms reveal the outcomes of meditating on God's Word?
12. How could Proverbs 2:1–5 serve as an excellent guide for someone learning to meditate on God's Word?
13. Using Isaiah 55:10–13 as a metaphor for the "normal" Christian life, what critical processes explained in Isaiah 55:1–10 must a person embrace?
14. Delight and joy in continual communion with Christ Jesus—is this expectation realistic in this world, or only a hope for heaven? What do the Scriptures describe as the optimal walk with Christ?
15. How has this study renewed your hope that you can become all God destined you to be?

Epilogue
What Difference Does It Make?

1. Have you ever discipled or mentored someone in their spiritual formation? If so, was your approach more "inside out" or "outside in"? What were the results?
2. Have you ever had someone tell you how to grow in Christ? Did you follow their advice? What were the results?
3. How does Peter's path empower you to have a genuine, personal relationship with Christ?
4. Why do you think the Author asked you to reflect on the questions: "Do you truly believe you care more about doing God's will than His Spirit, who dwells in you?" and "Do you think you care more about reaching people for Christ than the Savior who gave His life for them?" How did you answer?
5. Has this book given you hope for living an optimal and abundant life in Christ? Explain why or why not.

Made in the USA
Coppell, TX
24 August 2025